THE DIGITAL
CEO

A DOZEN YEARS OF IT INSIGHT

THE DIGITAL CEO

A DOZEN YEARS OF IT INSIGHT

BY

MARK HILLARY

The Digital CEO:
A Dozen Years Of IT Insight

© Mark Hillary and IBA Group Books 2021
All Rights Reserved

Published by
IBA Group Books
2583/13 Petržílkova St.
Prague 5, 158 00
Czech Republic

www.ibagroupit.com
https://blog.ibagroupit.com/

IBA Group Books
2583/13 Petržílkova St.
Prague 5, 158 00
Czech Republic

www.ibagroupit.com
https://blog.ibagroupit.com/

Author portrait supplied by the author.

Cover art by:

ISBN: 979 849 034 3165

The Digital CEO:
A Dozen Years Of IT Insight
© Mark Hillary and IBA Group Books 2021

This book is for Renata, Joe, and Ruby . . .

CONTENTS

ABOUT THE AUTHOR

Mark Hillary is a British technology writer and analyst, based in São Paulo, Brazil. He studied Software Engineering and has an MBA from the University of Liverpool.

Mark hosts the CX Files podcast with Peter Ryan–a weekly show focused on the future of customer experience. He frequently contributes to the global media, focused on technology and CX, with articles published by the BBC, Financial Times, Reuters, and Huffington Post.

Mark has written several books focused on technology. His first was titled 'Outsourcing to India: The Offshore Advantage' published in 2004 by Springer in Germany. He co-wrote 'Global Services: Moving To A Level Playing Field' with Dr Richard Sykes in 2007 for the British Computer Society and he translated all of Shakespeare's poetry into tweets in My Tweets Are Nothing Like The Sun: William Shakespeare on Twitter.

In 2021 he has published WFH: Securing The Future For Your Organization focused on the security of working from home and GigCX: Customer Service In The Twenty-First Century, focused on the emerging cloud based contact center industry.

Mark has lectured at or chaired major conferences in five continents and has extensive university experience as a guest MBA lecturer at London South Bank University for several years.

Mark has often been asked to help ghost-write speeches and articles for technology and CX leaders globally. In this capacity he has written for ambassadors, politicians, and CEOs across the world–helping them to deliver a clear message on the role of their company and industry.

Mark once spent a day helping Commander Neil Armstrong improve his standard 'going to the moon' speech so he could deliver his speech with added jokes about the telecoms industry–in front of 3,500 telecoms sales professionals it went fantastically well.

Mark has advised several national governments on technology policies and has advised the United Nations on the use of technology for development in Bangladesh and Nigeria.

http://bit.ly/markhillary
http://carnabysp.com
Social: @markhillary

FOREWORD

This book is inspired by many years of Mark's cooperation with IBA. I liked the idea to combine all blog publications on the latest technologies into a book and immediately decided to support it.

Mark began writing for our blog in 2010. In the first blog post, he said: "I'm Mark Hillary, a writer and blogger based in London, UK, and I'm going to explore some themes related to the global IT services industry on this blog."

Remarkably, he wrote about an economic crisis at that time: "The past couple of years have been a trying time for anyone involved in IT services. The global economic slowdown has affected most sectors, leaving few companies in a strong position, spending on IT for the future."

The today's pandemic triggered another economic crisis. However, the difference from 2008–2010 is that it did not slow down but accelerated technological advancements. The world became more reliant on IT. Technology changed the way we work, learn, shop, travel, and even the way we do our households.

Eventually, Mark relocated from London to São Paulo, Brazil. In parallel, he expanded the blog portfolio to reflect technology developments. We kept suggesting the technological topics related to our software expertise, and Mark analyzed and elaborated on those.

The range and grasp of his blog posts is amazing. I know that Mark graduated from a technology university. It was in the 1990s. I joined the IT industry even earlier. In the 1970s, I used to service computers that occupied several floors. Can you imagine that one rack of 1 Megabyte RAM memory weighed one ton?

I am fortunate to be a part of the exciting process of IT development. It has been a pleasure cooperating with Mark and I would like to invite you to go on a fascinating journey through the pages of this book, delving into new technologies and reflecting on our future.

Sergei Levteev
CEO, IBA Group
Prague, Czech Republic
October 2021

Go here to read all our articles in the IBA Group blog: https://blog.ibagroupit.com/

PREFACE AND INTRODUCTION

I n 2009, I visited a Gartner technology conference at a hotel close to Heathrow airport in London. I was chairing a panel discussion on technology and outsourcing in Eastern Europe in my role as a director of the UK National Outsourcing Association.

I met the IBA team because they had a stand at the event. I had written a few books on technology outsourcing so I asked them how business was going. After talking for a while I suggested that they might want to use some content as a way of promoting their business. This was several years before content marketing became essential for most technology companies.

The IBA team agreed, but in a different way to usual. When most companies ask me to write for them, they tell me the subject, who they are trying to interest, and any brands I should mention. Often, I will ghostwrite, rather than write something to be published in my own name, so I also need to know the style of the named author.

The IBA team just said, why don't you write some ideas about IT and we will publish them. Over the years they have suggested a few areas I might want to think about, but they have never said to me 'here is our latest service, please write about it.'

For a dozen years now I have been thinking about IT services and sending articles to IBA and they have been publishing them. It's been an interesting time in my life as I lived in my native London when I started on this journey and now I have a family in Brazil.

One of the reasons I have continued sending these ideas to IBA Group is because I like their approach to the IT industry. This business is full of hype. Fake it till you make it. Analysts like Gartner even regularly publish a 'hype cycle' reviewing which technologies might be real and which are just hot air.

The IBA Group approach has always been different. They get their head down and get on with the work. When I started talking to them about Robotic Process Automation (RPA)–at a time when most analysts were calling RPA hype–an engineer told me that his team had worked on over 300 project implementations. Who knew?

There is always a danger the IT experts that shout loudest are the ones that are always heard. Sometimes it pays to talk to the ones that are actually delivering IT projects, instead of loitering on LinkedIn "promoting" their expertise all day.

I hope this book goes some way to demonstrating that IBA Group has been ahead of the curve for many years. They were open to blogging and sharing ideas long before I started helping them and this open minded approach deserves more appreciation.

I'd like to thank Sergei Levteev and all his team at IBA Group as it's been a pleasure to build up this large volume of insight and observation. In particular I would like to thank the IBA Group Head of Corporate Communications, Irina Kiptikova, who was at the Gartner conference back in 2009 and has managed all of my contributions since then. The idea started at that conference and the IBA Group blog was launched in 2010.

This is not a definitive collection of all the articles published since 2010. Many are now outdated and some of them read better online, rather than in a book, so this is just a small selection from the past few years.

The past couple of years have been even more important than usual for the IT industry. It was the network and security engineers that enabled everyone to work from home during the Covid pandemic. The IT teams that built tools such as Zoom and Teams kept everyone connected for work and streaming services, such as Netflix and Disney+, kept everyone entertained when everything else was closed.

If this pandemic had occurred even a decade earlier it would have been far more difficult to cope with the sheer challenge of trying to keep companies running when people were not allowed to visit their workplace. Imagine a world where you are trapped at home without online games, Netflix, or Zoom.

It was the IT industry that saved so many companies during this crisis and now we are seeing a wave of accelerated digital transformation. Companies that were not forced to change for immediate survival have realized that consumer expectations have changed– they need to catch up.

I hope you enjoy these comments on different aspects of technology. If you have any comments or feedback then please feel free to contact me using the details on the author page.

Mark Hillary
São Paulo, Brazil
October 10, 2021

CHAPTER ONE

HOW IS OUTSOURCING BEING REDEFINED FOR THE FUTURE?

DECEMBER 4, 2017

Outsourcing has changed so much in the past decade. When my first book about outsourcing appeared in 2004 the emphasis was largely on the cost of delivering a service. Outsourcing was a strategy used mostly to reduce the cost of doing business.

That changed over time with flexibility and access to skills becoming as important, if not more, than the cost of service. But beyond this outsourcing has changed dramatically in the past decade. The way that companies work with each other, charge for services, and the way that services are delivered – it's all dramatically different now compared to the last decade.

Yet, when I browse the news I still run into articles like this.[1] Here there is a comparison between nearshoring to Eastern Europe and offshoring to India. There are differences between Europe and India, but the arguments in this articles don't really explore anything beyond saying that the IT companies in Europe are better, closer, and more reliable. It's the same argument that has been made in favor of nearshoring for about 20 years.

Now think about these three trends that are redefining how outsourcing really works:

1. **Delivery options;** are you delivering services via the cloud? Are you creating an app? Are you using Agile to create frequent upgrades?

2. **Payment options;** are you offering a freemium model where the client only pays for upgrades from a basic service? Are you offering a pay as you go model where the client can ramp up and down as they choose?

3. **Partnership;** the client is becoming the user and this changes the relationship from one with a master and servant to a much more equal need for partnership.

These are just three key areas of change, but they are important. The delivery model, the payment model, and the relationship between client and supplier are all dramatically changing from the types of outsourcing being described in the article I mentioned.

Most IT suppliers are changing fast. They have seen this change taking place in the market and they are working with their clients to deliver services using new methods. It's a shame that many in the trade and business press seem to still be talking about outsourcing as a way to save money, rather than a way to run your business.

CHAPTER TWO

WHY WON'T ROBOTS REPLACE HUMAN WORKERS?

MARCH 14, 2018

The business journals used to say that outsourcing and offshoring were replacing the need for companies to hire people. Now it's the robots that are supposed to be taking our jobs. Business journals and commentators across the world are suggesting that a wave of automation driven by smart Artificial Intelligence (AI) systems will largely replace the need for workers.

But what is the reality? Forrester Research does believe that a big change is coming, especially in highly developed markets like the US. Their latest study on the global workforce suggested that in 2018, 9% of US jobs will be lost to automation, partly offset by a 2% growth in jobs supporting this automation – the systems need to be managed. The most impacted areas will be back-office and administrative, sales, and call centre employees. A wide range of technologies, from Robotic Process Automation (RPA) and AI to customer self-service and physical robots will change how people are hired and will create a need for different skills.

Analysis by McKinsey is cautious. They warn that just because it is technically feasible for tasks to be automated does not mean that every company will do so. This is similar to the earlier concerns about outsourcing. It is technically feasible to outsource almost every function of a company, yet few companies outsource everything.

McKinsey says that when planning what is possible to automate, first you need to rate jobs and tasks by their technical feasibility – is this a repetitive process that a robot or software bot could perform? For example, when thinking about manual work tasks such as a factory assembly line or food packaging are predictable and it is possible to consider how these tasks could be automated. Construction, forestry, or working with animals is highly unstructured and not predictable and therefore almost impossible to automate.

Let's consider a simple example. IBA Group created an email bot that sorts incoming emails at the customer support centres.[1] The EmailBot processes typical customer requests, grouping these by content, sending automatic responses, creating tickets, and gathering statistics. However, even a constantly-learning robot cannot process all customer requests. Roughly 50-70 percent of incoming emails are processed automatically and the rest are forwarded to the appropriate employees. Nevertheless, in this case the employees are relieved from repetitive operations and are able to focus on more complicated tasks so value is created.

But factories and manufacturing are just one part of the economy. In most developed economies services are a greater part of the economy. Here there are clear examples of how some automation can be introduced.

Look at how customers in McDonald's are now comfortable using a screen to order their own meal. Amazon has proven that an entire supermarket can be automated[2], so not even checkouts are required.

Computer Weekly recently published an interesting study of automation that draws the conclusion that the real story is not that robots will cause jobs to vanish. Some jobs will go, but millions will also be created because of the automation. The real story is that many of the jobs we are familiar with today will be transformed.[3]

This rings true. Think about the skills needed by a finance assistant or Human Resources professional in an environment where many business processes will be automated. These office professionals need to be able to control the automation systems and improve them – the back office professionals you are now hiring probably need to be able to code software. That never used to be a requirement in HR, but it will be soon.

The McKinsey research analyses over 800 different types of job and explores the possibility of robots replacing these tasks. You can read the research here[4], but to my mind it is the transformation of skills that is the real story – not robots replacing workers. Workers need to understand how to work with the robots and control them so they can be more productive.

CHAPTER THREE

HOW THE ROBOTS IN YOUR HOME ARE CREATING NEW OPPORTUNITIES

MAY 16, 2018

I recently bought a Furbo. It's a device that started life on the crowdfunding platform Indiegogo. You fill the Furbo with small dog treats and when away from home it's possible to watch your dog using the camera and toss those treats remotely. It's also possible to speak and listen to what your dog is 'saying'.

It's just a fun device, but it is also one more connection to the Internet. Our homes are becoming filled with connected devices and slowly our home environment is becoming far more technology-enabled than any office, where the focus is still on connecting little more than computers and printers.

Think about your own home environment. Do you have an Amazon Echo or Google Home system? That means you will have connected microphones dotted around the house. What about your phone, laptop, and Kindle? If you have a games console that that will also be connected and how else can your TV access Netflix if that's not online?

Much of the traditional media we used to consume in the home such as records, movies, and books is now consumed electronically. We stream Netflix to a Smart TV. We stream Spotify music to a home theatre or speaker system. We download books and magazines to e-readers like the Amazon Kindle. The connected home has slowly become a reality and is no longer unusual or cutting edge.

Data published last year by Cisco estimates that by 2021 each person in North America will be using 13 connected devices.[1] Thirteen for each person! That's a lot of Kindles and Furbos.

Naturally much of this growth is because everyday objects are gradually becoming connected. It would be unusual to buy a new car today and to find that it does not ask to connect to your wifi. Tesla cars regularly upgrade themselves when parked overnight. A new channel between products and their manufacturer has been created allowing automated updates and maintenance to take place without user involvement.

Smart leaders need to look beyond the devices and think about the data. When people are streaming constant information on their location and behavior how can your business tap into that information to create genuine value? Insurance companies are one great example of a sector that is benefitting from this move to an Internet of Things (IoT) environment. If a car driver only pays insurance for their car when it is used and they are rewarded for safe driving behavior then that helps the customer and the insurance company. Insurance is being redefined by this real-time data on the customer.

How is your business reacting to this connected environment? Can you see the opportunities or does it just seem like a threat to the established way of doing business?

CHAPTER FOUR

AI IS BRINGING BRANDS AND CONSUMERS CLOSER TOGETHER

SEPTEMBER 18, 2018

Artificial Intelligence (AI) is quite a pervasive technology in the present-day environment. Even regular consumers with no technical knowledge are becoming aware of AI and are comfortable interacting with these systems. Examples are all around, from Siri on the Apple iPhone to the movie recommendations made by Netflix and song playlists on Spotify.

But there are many other ways in which consumers are beginning to interact with AI systems and many of them are not so obvious, at least to the end consumer of the services.[1] Think of self-driving cars. They may not be common yet, but they are being tested all over the world and they rely on AI to constantly monitor the environment outside the car and to decide what to do next to keep the vehicle safe.

AI can also help to predict what people will do in the future. Facebook can tell if you are likely to take your own life based on recent posts. Stanford University trained a system to detect if you are gay or straight based just facial photographs. The HR system designed by IBM can predict who is likely to quit their job. The implications for these insights are fairly clear – imagine what an insurance company or government could do with this data.

Perhaps more positively, there are now investment algorithms that outperform regular investment managers and AI-powered disease diagnosis means that your virtual doctor will be aware of any relevant research and drug trials – even if it was just published yesterday.

Most consumers will be largely unaware of these developments, but there is one area where people are creating a huge demand for greater investment and research into AI systems and that is personalization – the interaction between consumers and brands.

Years ago it was Amazon that really started this wave of personalization by offering deals or recommendations based on the specific shopping behavior of the individual customer. This was extremely innovative at the time because most brands could only ever offer the same deal to all customers at the same time. Now this is commonplace and expected.

A clothes retailer needs to know what the customer likes, dislikes, their shopping history, and what they have browsed and lingered over in the past. All these insights would be impossible for a person, but an AI system can figure out what to offer the customer – either as a recommendation or as a special offer – and ensure that the offer is made at exactly the time that the customer is most likely to respond positively.

Now these personalized insights are not only becoming more common, but customers know that brands have the data so they are expecting greater personalization. Customer demand is creating a wave of

IT research and development. AI is moving quickly from being interesting and innovative to becoming essential for brands across many industries and it is customer expectation that is driving this change.

CHAPTER FIVE

WHEN WILL YOUR HR TEAM START LEARNING TO CODE?

OCTOBER 17, 2018

There are many emerging technologies that are not only changing the workplace, but changing the way that jobs are structured and the skills that modern (or future) employees need. I believe that three of the most important changes taking place at present include:

1. Artificial Intelligence (AI) in the workplace
2. Remote working
3. Creating tribes

There are technologies and systems emerging, such as AI in business application support, that are fundamentally changing how corporate processes function – and this changes the skills that people in professional jobs need.[1] Employees need to become comfortable with the idea of AI delivering performance feedback, personal development, coaching and evaluation. This offers many advantages to both employee and employer, but it can still face resistance by some employees, especially when they feel it will change their job.

Forbes magazine recently published data from a study by the Center for Effective Organizations at USC Marshall School of Business. The study suggested that only 37% of employees would share innovation or automation ideas if they believed they would have to do different work as a result of such technology being implemented. However, when employees believed the technology would help make their job better, 87% of them said they would share innovation ideas with their employer.

Both AI and employees will help companies to reengineer their processes, but with AI exploring how to optimize systems there is an opportunity to change processes without the natural reluctance of the employees.

Remote working is increasingly a reality in many industries. Customer service companies are now actively promoting the Work-At-Home-Agent model instead of increasingly large contact centers. Companies with a large number of home-based employees can dramatically reduce costs for office estate and more easily scale up and down as the business requires.

The need to create tribes is partly related to the trend for home-working, but it is also linked to our increasing use of social networks. As we see people less in real life and more in virtual spaces, such as social networks, it becomes more important to be more methodical about socializing – both in person and virtually.

All these changes in the way we work are related back to the increasing intelligence of systems that can help us to perform more effectively at work. We are now reaching a point where coding skills are becoming useful for employees in almost any professional job –

accounting, HR, and law companies will all be using AI business application support and this means that professionals need to learn how to manage their virtual tools.

A great change is coming soon. It's not that every job will vanish as many are automated, but those that remain will become more interesting and more technical – the HR team needs to start coding soon!

CHAPTER SIX

HOW TECH PLAYS AN IMPORTANT ROLE IN DELIVERING GREAT CX

JANUARY 11, 2019

I recently visited IBA Group in Minsk[1] and I had the pleasure to speak with Andrei Lepeyev, the director of software development at IBA Group. As someone who studied software engineering at university myself, I'm always fascinated by the way that platforms such as cloud computing and the app store have changed what it means to deliver software, so it was really great to catch up with Andrei.

You can hear our conversation on the CX Files podcast by clicking here[2] or search your favorite audio podcast provider, such as iTunes, Spotify, SoundCloud, or Stitcher. Because we were focused on CX we talked about some of the technologies and systems that Andrei is working on that have a direct impact on the quality of CX for the clients of IBA Group.

I had initially asked Andrei about how Artificial Intelligence (AI) is being used to predict customer behavior, but he explained to me that IBA has gone further and created a product called APPULSE that offers a complete Level 1 and 2 support service for mainframe computer systems.

Andrei said: "APPULSE not only detects the system and finds problems, it uses Machine Learning to learn about the solutions so in many cases it can create a self-healing mainframe system. Mainframes are still really important and unbeaten in the range of directions they are deployed. They are the most stable and virus-free systems, but their user-interface is not usually so good."

Andrei was talking about the importance of keeping mainframes running because they are often overlooked by most customers, yet your bank will be relying on those systems to be running if they want to offer a 24/7 online banking platform. Ensuring that the system can heal itself before problems even happen is an enormous improvement in the way that a traditional IT support operation would run – fixing problems only after they have caused a problem. That's always a disaster for customers who need service now.

One of the big trends for 2019 in CX will be Robotic Process Automation (RPA). Andrei explained to me that IBA Group has delivered implementations all over the world using the top four RPA platforms[3] so they are not just riding a wave of RPA hype, they have real customers and case studies from numerous countries. But I asked Andrei how they choose the best platform for different customers – is the software really very different?

He said: "First we think about the support level of each supplier. Can they provide education or trial systems? Can they add specific requests to the software? Can they give extra information to a company like ours that may be implementing the solution?" However Andrei also added an interesting point which is not often discussed in the industry – sometimes it is just which software system is seen first by the customer. He said: "It is also important to see how each of the companies is marketing their product to the client. Often we will be approached by a potential client who already has a pilot system – developed free by the software vendor – and it can be very hard to move them to another system even if we think it could be better."

Andrei mentioned Machine Learning when describing the mainframe support system and I asked him about the popularity of this in 2019. Are more and more customers asking how to make their systems learn about customers and systems automatically?

Andrei said: "Yes, many more clients are asking about it. The main reason is that there has been an evolution of hardware. A simple mobile phone allows almost every standard machine learning platform to work. Ten years ago this was impossible. We are not talking about huge brands like Google and Amazon – even smaller companies can deploy a machine learning system today – there is a very low barrier to entry now."

When I asked Andrei about his priorities for 2019 he said that he wanted everyone in the industry to remember that none of these technologies exist in a vacuum – they all need to interact with other technologies and business processes. He said: "When we are talking about AI we cannot talk about it alone, it should be the business application of AI. We can't talk about RPA without Machine Learning. We can't talk about Cloud Computing without talking about the solutions that are built and deployed on the cloud. I'm looking forward to some projects in 2019 that involve AI using RPA and are delivered on the cloud."

My conversation with Andrei provided a great insight into how some of these technologies are really affecting the customer experience. A large amount of media coverage is just hype, but as Andrei demonstrated, there is a great deal of substance here. These technologies can deliver game-changing systems, but the companies using them to interact with their customers need to have great products and services – it is not the use of an RPA or AI platform alone that will help them to be more successful.

CHAPTER SEVEN

HOW DO YOU UNDERSTAND WHAT CUSTOMERS WILL WANT IN THE FUTURE?

MAY 2, 2019

It was great to read the article published on the IBA Group website about the CXOutsourcers Mindshare event in Windsor, UK.[1] This was a very interesting event hosted by Peter Ryan and Mark Angus connecting together the service providers from the BPO (Business Process Outsourcing) and CX (Customer Experience) industry.

The IBA team was there at the event because their expertise in areas such as Cloud Computing and Robotic Process Automation is highly in demand from the CX companies – hopefully they managed to strike a few new partnerships!

As mentioned in the IBA article, I was speaking at the event about the future of the customer experience – how can you profile and understand the customer of the future?

What I tried to do with this talk was to initially frame expectations. It is easy for people to make wild predictions about how customers will behave in future, but what they often forget is that social and technological progress is not always gradual. Sometimes an invention or innovation can completely change the way that people behave.

A good way to think of this is by considering how railways changed society. Before railways people were forced to live within walking distance of their workplace. Railways created the freedom for people to travel to work and this in turn created the concept of the suburb.

We have seen a similar change in the past decade. Since the launch of the Apple iPhone in 2007 and the subsequent explosion in the use of social networks, the way that people communicate with each other has dramatically changed. This has led to a radical change in the way that people communicate with brands and an evolution in the way that the customer journey works – this is the journey from first hearing of a product to learning more and then eventually buying it.

That customer journey used to be quite simple and was focused on advertising or marketing to create awareness and then a sales process followed by customer support. Now we can see brands that are not building customer service contact centers, they are building customer experience hubs. They are using a mix of human and digital technologies and building an ongoing relationship with customers that can last for half a century or more.

What is so interesting about the present day business environment is that there is so much potential for dramatic change in so many ways. A retailer planning strategy in the era of my parents would only ever be planning new store locations and sales promotions – nothing in the future was dramatically different to the past.

Look at the retail environment today. Not only is online retail creating a new era of competition, but the way that town centers are featuring retail is changing. Other huge factors may also change how society interacts with business, such as climate change, geopolitics and the dramatic rise of China, the creation of social inequalities, and the preference to rent experiences rather than owning products.

You can click the link to read through my slides[2] for some more of the ideas I presented at CXOutsourcers, but I think that what we will see more often today is emerging business models and services driven by the online economy and the desire of the customer for greater convenience. Go-Jek in Indonesia started out as a ride-hailing service with motorbikes – like Uber with two wheels. They expanded into offering services such as medicine or food delivery by leveraging their network of riders and eventually they created such a wide array of services that they introduced their own in-app payment system. They now process more payments than any major credit card brand . . . they are now a financial service brand and they started out offering rides on scooters.

How might this happen in your industry? Think about it, your competition in 2020 may not even exist today or they may be working in a completely different industry. Now that's scary because it means that we are moving faster than ever to stay ahead of business trends, but we are never going to be going this slow again in future.

CHAPTER EIGHT

HOW IS ARTIFICIAL INTELLIGENCE DEVELOPING IN THE ENTERPRISE?

MAY 14, 2019

Artificial Intelligence (AI) has moved from science fiction into the enterprise in recent years. Many companies are using AI systems today to intelligently analyze large volumes of changing data and to notice or predict patterns. Typical business uses today include examples such as:

- Rail operators predicting train delays before they happen because the AI system can extrapolate from small delays to predict the impact on the entire network.
- Customer service agents being advised on how to help customers by systems that know the answer to every question a customer has asked in the past.
- Alexa knows how to answer your question[1] because it immediately processes your voice and determines what you are asking before creating an answer.

- Netflix knows which movie you might want to watch because they know your past behavior and how similar customers have also behaved.

AI really is all around us today, in the enterprise and as consumers of services. In the present environment it would now be unusual for any company to not be exploring how AI can improve their business.

But AI does have one a fundamental flaw, it is always limited to working on a very specific problem. This means that you can have a very complex system that knows everything that your customer may ask when they call for help or the system may understand how to play chess or Go, but these individual tasks are all that it can do. There is no inherent awareness of the environment around the system – although we use the term intelligence, it's not really aware or sentient. An AI system that can play Go cannot plan the best route on a map.

This means that the system can only solve the problems it was designed for. Some might argue that this is a benefit, because it means that however good our AI systems get, they never move into the realm of awareness and all the problems that a conscious system might create.

A recent experiment by IBM[2] has demonstrated that AI is developing rapidly though. They demonstrated how an AI system could be asked a random question and it would then have the ability to debate that subject. For example, in the video clip that I watched the system was asked if pre-school facilities should be subsidized by the government. It gave a response, arguing why subsidies are useful for 4 minutes.

This system has been pre-loaded with information on millions of subjects and objects. It's stuffed full of encyclopedia content and research. But even with all this data it is quite an achievement to turn that into information and then a coherent argument.

Essentially this system is starting to show that perhaps an Artificial General Intelligence might be possible. It would need to be pre-loaded with an enormous amount of general data, and then would need a Machine Learning system to continue learning, but it is looking more feasible than even a year or two ago when Elon Musk started warning[3] that we are heading for an 'AI apocalypse' because the machines will eventually have more intelligence than the humans.

I don't think we will be seeing many business case studies featuring general intelligence just yet, but AI in the form we already know it will certainly be more important. AI is offering companies a chance to identify patterns and trends they could never see manually and this will be a strong source of competitive advantage in the next few years.

CHAPTER NINE

HOW IS RPA INNOVATION TAKING SHAPE?

JUNE 11, 2019

I have written in the past about how impressed I was when I visited IBA Group in person.[1] They don't really shout about it, but their Robotic Process Automation (RPA) team has a level of expertise that I was not expecting to find when I visited Minsk last December. I keep recalling this when I see some of the analyst and media coverage of RPA online because there is still a strange mixture of anticipation and hype in most of the analysis.

HfS Research has been one of the main critics of the hype around RPA. They have consistently called on other analysts to provide realistic market projections and to stop using the 'robots are taking over' myths that have grown in frequency in the past two years. Their Horse For Sources blog in particular has been scathing when individual analysts have made RPA claims that just cannot be supported by evidence or case studies.

HfS has documented that they believe the 'big 3' RPA companies–Automation Anywhere, Blue Prism, and UiPath–are creating a baseline for the entire industry.[2] It's messy out there because there are loads of companies that are trying to get a piece of the RPA hype and yet not everyone can succeed–not least because each system needs experienced people who can implement and use it. I believe that WorkFusion should also be on this list as they are not only creating a baseline, but they are disrupting the marketing by even offering basic RPA services free.[3]

On March 3rd the Horses For Sources blog said this: "However, beyond scripts and bots and dreams of digital workers scaling up rapidly to provide reams of value, most enterprises are fast coming to the realization that they need an actual process automation platform capability that ingests their data, visualizes it, machine learns it, contextualizes it and finally automates it."[4]

The blog goes on to say: "The implication is that for many companies the dream is over. They thought that RPA would work easily and yet they have found that it's actually quite complex to integrate into their main business processes. You cannot just point an RPA system at a business and say 'automate that' in the same way that computer software doesn't write itself–someone needs to understand how to code so the computer understands what you need."

Go and follow the references above if you want to read the conclusion to what they think will happen next, although the short story is that they believe that there may be a new phase of RPA led by AntWorks [5] with a more integrated approach to automation. In a way, we are seeing the process of automation becoming more automated.

I think there are two conclusions that can be drawn from what we are seeing in the RPA market at present. First is that most implementations are started to coalesce around the three top system suppliers and that's a good thing because the market cannot tolerate the fragmentation that dozens of small systems creates. Second, the RPA story is not over yet. It remains quite difficult to implement and anyone making this process easier could well lead the next chapter in the RPA story.

CHAPTER TEN

WHAT IS A CLOUD MANAGEMENT PLATFORM?

JUNE 19, 2019

Most people working in IT today know about the cloud and how cloud-based systems can offer immediate access to storage or computing power easily. Many companies now use a cloud strategy to ensure they can ramp up and down on available systems or storage—it's a common theme of discussion when planning an IT strategy.

But what is a Cloud Management Platform and in particular how can one be useful to service providers offering IT services to their clients?

Cloud Management Platform (CMP) is a term coined by the industry analyst Gartner. The analyst firm wanted a way to describe products or tools that help companies to optimize and manage their cloud infrastructure for cost, security, and operations. A good CMP strategy should allow users to maintain control over dynamic and scalable cloud environments.

So it is really just a control system that allows the user to maintain dynamic control over their cloud system. Instead of frantically calling a service provider and asking them to quickly scale up storage capacity in their contracted cloud, the customer should be able to use a CMP to just scale their cloud–it should be as easy as sliding a bar on a control panel.

The major CMPs on the market today will all offer these different aspects of cloud management:

- Cost
- Security
- Performance

These are the three main areas where the customer can manage their cloud and cover more specific areas such as budgeting, rightsizing the cloud, compliance and monitoring, and creating alerts and other analytics.

CMPs are still quite new tools and so there are still different types of tool available. Some are very focused on specific issues, such as controlling security risk or optimizing costs. Some allow the option to manage multiple clouds, so if you are using both Microsoft Azure and Amazon AWS then you can manage both clouds from a single tool. Some CMPs even allow the tool to manage a cloud and systems you have on site simultaneously.

Clearly this is an emerging area. There are many new tools solving problems that have only recently become apparent. It was only a few years back that companies started taking cloud-based services seriously and it has become clear that it can be difficult to control the various aspects of a cloud-based system–such as cost control and security. In addition, if a service provider is delivering services on a cloud that is owned and managed by the client then the client needs an easy way to manage areas such as security in partnership with their service provider.

CMPs are still new and it is therefore difficult to advise on which one is perfect for each client, but there is a clear need to work on CMP selection with your service provider as any chosen solution must work for both client and service provider. I'll explore this question next time here on the IBA Group blog.

CHAPTER ELEVEN

HOW DO I CHOOSE A CLOUD MANAGEMENT PLATFORM?

JULY 9, 2019

I introduced the concept of a Cloud Management Platform (CMP) in my last article here on the IBA Group blog and closed by saying that it's a complex process to choose a specific platform. However, that's exactly the decision that many managers are exploring right now and it can be even more complex when you need to buy a cloud, but it is your service provider that will actually be using it.

This white paper from the IT research firm Neovise[1] gives some excellent advice on this particular issue. The white paper introduces the need for CMPs, as I did in my last article, but then it lists some specific questions you need to ask when determining the best system to use:

1. **Business Requirements:**
    *   What customers do you plan to serve, and what are their requirements? How well will the cloud platform serve them?

- How much additional work is required for installation/configuration? Integration? Adding missing features?
- How quickly will the cloud platform let you get to market and start generating revenue?

2. **Product Requirements:**
   - Does the platform enable the right compute, network and storage capabilities?
   - Are there specific hardware requirements for the platform? Or can you choose hardware from any vendor? Can you leverage existing hardware investments?
   - How extensible is the product? Does it support federation with other providers?
   - Does the platform allow you to seamlessly integrate new cloud services with your existing hosting services?

3. **Support Requirements:**
   - Will it require significant resources and expertise to deploy, customize and operate the platform?
   - What do you do if you need help deploying or troubleshooting the platform? Is there customer support? Or just community support? Both?
   - Does the platform receive ongoing enhancements? Are new versions difficult or disruptive to install?

These are quite detailed questions and there are different types of CMP as I outlined in my earlier article, but if you go into these questions with a clear outline of your specific capabilities, resource, timeline, and strategy then you can achieve a successful outcome. It's recommended to include this information on any RFI or RFP process when selecting a supplier so you can work with a supplier that supports your preferences on CMP in addition to just agreeing on a cloud strategy.

Where you have not already deployed a cloud or CMP then it would be preferable to outline your preferences and needs right from the RFI–this way a potential partner can advise on the best cloud to use and the best tools to manage it.

In the early days of cloud adoption this was all easier. A client would just make requests directly to their supplier if more capacity or storage is needed, but as IT infrastructure has become more complex, and usually involves a mix of cloud and on premises equipment, it is essential to make the right choices about the system you use to manage your cloud–and manage it in a way that works with the needs of your supplier.

CHAPTER TWELVE

EVEREST REPORTS ON A COMPLEX AND COMPETITIVE RPA MARKET

JULY 31, 2019

The industry analyst firm Everest Group recently reported their latest research into the development of the Robotic Process Automation (RPA) market and they have some interesting findings. The market is getting larger and more competitive, but the services provided are also increasing in complexity too.[1]

"The market for RPA technology is becoming more complex, with highly competitive and evolving product offerings," said Sarah Burnett, executive vice president and distinguished analyst at Everest Group. "The Everest Group Products PEAK Matrix is an unbiased assessment that uncovers vendor and product differentiators to identify the leaders in RPA technology based on research that goes deep into the vendors performance and product details, features, functionalities and more."

The PEAK Matrix reporting method summarizes the 22 companies studied along two different axes. The first is vision and quality, describing the ability of the company to successfully deliver the products they promise. The second is the market impact, how is their sales performance and impact on the wider RPA marketplace?

Everest Group classified the main RPA technology vendors into three categories of Leaders, Major Contenders, and Aspirants:

- **Leaders:** Automation Anywhere, Blue Prism, NICE and UiPath
- **Major Contenders:** Another Monday, AntWorks, EdgeVerve, HelpSystems, Jacada, Jidoka, Kofax, Kryon, Pegasystems, Servicetrace, Softomotive, Thoughtonomy and WorkFusion
- **Aspirants:** AutomationEdge, Datamatics, Intellibot, Nintex and Nividous

AntWorks, Automation Anywhere, Datamatics, Softomotive and UiPath demonstrated the strongest year-over-year movement on both market impact and vision-and-capability dimensions and emerged as "2019 RPA Market Star Performers." WorkFusion scored as high, or higher sometimes, on the vision and quality measurement as the leaders, but it was felt that they have not quite made the market impact to be categorized as a leader – yet.

Other interesting takeaways from the Everest research include:

- Automation Anywhere, Blue Prism, and UiPath are the top vendors in terms of RPA license revenue, closely followed by NICE. Pegasystems leads in terms of revenue from attended RPA (RDA) licenses
- Softomotive has the highest number of RPA clients in the market, most of which are small-

sized enterprises and SMBs. Witnessing almost 300% year-over-year growth in its number of clients, UiPath holds the second spot in terms of number of RPA clients

- Automation Anywhere leads in North America, which is the largest RPA market, and Latin America. Blue Prism leads in the UK and MEA markets, while UiPath leads in Continental Europe and Asia Pacific
- UiPath holds the highest market share by license revenue across horizontal functions such as F&A, procurement, and HR, while Blue Prism leads in banking and insurance industry-specific process areas. Pegasystems has the highest market share in the contact centre space
- Leaders have moved away from perpetual licensing to annual/monthly subscription-based licensing models. Advances in RPA technologies and increasing client maturity are fueling the rise of more output-oriented pricing models such as flexible usage-based (e.g., per minute/hour) and per-process or transaction-based models
- RPA solutions continue to evolve with a host of capabilities, such as computer vision, workflow orchestration, intelligent workload balancing, auto-scalability, and predictive SLA monitoring, to help enterprises achieve strategic business outcomes
- Attended RPA / RDA continues to witness increased demand in the market. AI-based next-best-action recommendation and interactive UI for on-screen agent guidance, which enhance worker productivity and help improve customer experience, are among the key RDA differentiators

This new research from Everest Group is comprehensive and insightful and was only just published in July 2019 so the information is current. I recommend browsing their findings because it is clear that RPA has moved beyond the hype cycle now and is becoming a serious strategy for many company executives.

CHAPTER THIRTEEN

WHAT ARE THE TOP CLOUD MANAGEMENT PLATFORMS?

AUGUST 15, 2019

In my last couple of articles here I explored Cloud Management Platforms (CMP)[1], both to define what they are and to give some ideas on how to choose the best one for a particular business. It was therefore interesting to see that a recent article in ITPro Today explores the top ten CMPs available today, assessing all their strengths and weaknesses.[2]

All CMPs need to provide lifecycle management – this is the ability to track cloud resources over a period of time – and data protection, in addition to the main functionality of controlling and automating cloud-based processes. John Webster, a senior partner and analyst at the Evaluator Group, managed the research published in ITPro Today.[3] One of his main concerns when comparing the different CMPs was that not all of them are keenly focused on data protection – they are focusing mainly on basic functionality.

John explained: "Data protection and disaster recovery is an IT responsibility, a bedrock function, and

I think that the vendors in this space have to really start looking at that seriously." He added: "Vendors will likely provide these capabilities through extensions to data protection and disaster recovery applications that are already available in the market."

The top ten list of CMPs was created by weighing up several factors, including:

- The quality of the user interface
- Ability to manage various groups of users
- Complexity of the service

Cost control is an important area of functionality that most customers want to use, but many CMP vendors find it very difficult to offer because they are constantly updating their products. The ability to create efficiency is much easier to plan when the software is stable. If the CMP is constantly being improved then there is an almost constant need to explore efficiencies.

John explained that support for Artificial Intelligence (AI) is likely to be an important capability in the near future. He said: "Support for cloud-native including Kubernetes, and application migration will be key functions in cloud management platform tools. AI assistance, or the assistance of artificial intelligence, will become more and more important as time goes on."

Some of the CMPs on the market at present have been built from trusted and tested systems that were essentially managing IT estates – they have been converted to managing cloud-based systems, but others are built from scratch. It's important to be aware of this when selecting a supplier. The start-ups might move faster and add more features all the time, but their platforms may be less stable and less tested in real-life situations.

The ten CMPs are not listed with the best in position one; they are just grouped as the ten best CMPs. This is because ultimately the right choice of CMP will be based on the different priorities and needs of each company. Follow the link to the article and you can read the top ten free, providing you submit your contact details to the magazine.

CHAPTER FOURTEEN

WHY SHOULD I BE THINKING ABOUT DEVOPS?

SEPTEMBER 16, 2019

What is DevOps? If you don't directly work on the development of IT systems then this might be a strange concept, but for any executive who needs to purchase new technology systems, or modify existing ones, this is an important concept to be aware of.

In short, DevOps refers to Development Operations. It is a combined set of software development practices that bring together the development of software with the with IT operations. The aim is to create an environment where the systems development lifecycle can be shorter and more features and updates can be performed – in general it aims to bring IT development much closer to the business that is being served.

The broad goals span the entire lifecycle of a software project:

- Increased frequency of project deliveries
- Faster time to market on the original delivery

- Lower failure rate of delivered software
- Shorter lead time between business requests and fixes being applied
- Faster recovery time when failure does occur

By using a DevOps approach the IT team can maximize the predictability of new releases. Efficiency and security are both increased and the code becomes easier to maintain.

The IBA Group has conducted research into the effect of using a DevOps approach to software development – although this research was focused on mainframe DevOps. These are some of the key findings:

- 20 x faster to recover when software fails
- 22% less time spent on rework to fix problems
- 30 x more deployments of new software
- 40 x lower failure rate of delivered software
- 50 x greater IT team satisfaction

All this data comes from real mainframe client projects at IBA Group. Deployment becomes more reliable and more frequent when people work together using this type of framework. The IT team uses a form of system thinking, which really means that they create a culture of shared responsibility for the project. This culture encourages transparency and shared responsibility – problems that one team member may have hidden in a regular organization are shared and managed together.

Automation is also an important part of the DevOps culture. The aim is to automate all the routine tasks a developer usually needs to manage. This also creates a far more satisfied developer who can focus on the more interesting and challenging parts of the project. This naturally leads to better quality and performance – enhancing the reputation of the team.

Most executives outside IT are not really familiar with software development practices, but it is becoming more important to understand because a different approach to the way that software development is managed leads directly to business effects, such as better quality, fewer failures, and a team with higher satisfaction in their job. DevOps is well established as a practice with a decade of conferences and articles all exploring how it can be used effectively. If you need to purchase any form of software development from an IT company then how they are managing DevOps should be one of the first things you ask.

CHAPTER FIFTEEN

A RENEWED FOCUS ON CLOUD SECURITY

SEPTEMBER 30, 2019

Capital One bank in the US was recently targeted by a single hacker who managed to access the personal details of over 100 million customers, despite the bank having all the security you might expect of a large customer-focused organization.[1] The hacker was a former employee of Amazon Web Services (AWS), which hosted the bank database. They broke in by exploiting a poorly configured firewall, no doubt using some of their inside knowledge.

Once again we are watching as a major brand faces a data disaster. Capital One should be able to absorb the millions of dollars in fines and customer compensation, but for a smaller organization this type of data breach could be the end. European fines are much higher than those in the US thanks to the European Union GDPR regulation, but why should companies be more focused on this question of data security now?

Because of cloud computing. A recent report in CIO suggested that 96% of companies are now using cloud computing.[2] This means that almost every new database will be in the cloud. Justin Fier, the director of cyber-intelligence at Darktrace recently suggested that the general approach to securing networks – mainly with firewalls – has not yet woken up to the fact that everything is now in the cloud.[3]

Network security managers have spent years designing their systems with the concept of what is inside the organization, what is outside, and how to protect network entry points. Now we are seeing a complete shift away from this structure to the cloud. Companies such as Microsoft and Amazon are offering cloud services that allow their customers to access unlimited storage and computing power.

But this also means that your personal customer data will be outside the organization and physically located on a service managed by another company. Companies like Amazon have developed a reputation for security and are probably better at securing their systems than any old internal system you previously had, but what happens when a current or former employee goes rogue and hacks into the database they used to manage?

As Justin Fier suggests, there are some new approaches to data management and network security that are essential:

- Better network oversight; your development and support team can probably create and use new servers instantly meaning that the security team often has no real oversight on the network that is really being used. Give them better tools that allow them to manage what is really out there on the network.
- Look for malware; Capital One only ever found out about the hack, three months after it happened, because stolen data was seen

online. Be proactive and seek out malware and other tricks that hackers will use to break in.

- Explore Artificial Intelligence (AI); you often can't prevent an insider launching an attack so create some digital oversight. Use an AI system to monitor all network activity so you can be alerted when any unusual activity takes place – and ensure that nobody can turn off this AI police officer.

The bottom line is that cloud computing offers too many advantages and opportunities for companies to avoid it. With an adoption rate that is now almost universal there is no going back, but we certainly need to consider how best to change and adjust network security for the cloud computing era.

The border or the organization is no longer the office itself. People and their skills are sourced from suppliers and databases will be located in the cloud. Both people and data now move in and out of the central organization in a porous way. Protecting this environment is the challenge we face today. Questions about a cloud security strategy should be amongst the first things any executive should be asking any potential IT partner and if the supplier fails to have any intelligent answers then why would you work together?

CHAPTER SIXTEEN

EMERGING COMPETITION IN EUROPEAN IT OUTSOURCING

OCTOBER 1, 2019

Emerging Europe is a great business journal for anyone with an interest in Central and Eastern Europe. The journal covers every aspect of business and economics in the region and often covers the IT and Business Process Outsourcing developments in the region.[1]

Naturally this is an important industry because the concept of European nearshoring is now quite mature. Companies in western Europe, such as the UK and Germany, have built strong relationships with companies in the East that offer particular expertise – often at a lower price than that possible in the west.

I recently read a feature in the journal that explores how European outsourcing is changing. The focus is on some emerging markets and how their attractiveness is changing the locations where some companies will consider offshoring. In particular some markets such as Poland, Bulgaria, and Moldova are described as fast growing.

However, once again the focus here is on cost. The sales pitch for Moldova is that it is a cheaper location to operate than either Romania or Bulgaria and junior software developers can be hired for as little as 300 Euros a month.

IT companies, consultants, and industry analysts have spent at least the past twenty years making these comparisons and talking about the next CEE location to emerge, but I think that by now we should know enough about IT delivery to no longer be focused on the cost of an individual software developer. IT companies in Europe are offering highly specialized services and any company today that is still exploring outsourcing as a slash and burn strategy is probably doomed to failure.

The entire IT industry has changed beyond recognition in the past decade and this has led to a fundamental shift in how projects are delivered and used. Consumers have become entirely familiar with the concept of the app store. They are comfortable selecting new software for their devices and installing it. People often forget that until Apple changed the smartphone market, you bought a phone and could then only use the software that was installed at the time of purchase. The end user couldn't change anything.

So the way that consumer software is bought and used has completely changed in just a few short years, but the enterprise has also seen a similar change. Many organizations now use the app store concept as a way to distribute systems, allowing individual employees to setup and manage the systems they need to use.

In addition, the explosion in cloud computing has meant that many enterprise systems are now accessed using the cloud and only paid for as they are used. This has also changed the IT budgeting process. Many companies use the cloud for all their enterprise systems meaning that they pay for only what they use, when they use it, and it is the business line manager – not the CIO – that is paying the bill.

So when we talk about low cost software developers in Moldova, who is really hiring them because most companies have entirely changed their IT and sourcing strategy. Companies offering IT expertise in the CEE region cannot survive in this environment by saying they employ the cheapest expertise. They need to be offering cloud-based solutions, customization to existing ERP and CRM systems, services related to the design and installation of Robotic Process Automation (RPA).

The way that almost every company uses IT has changed completely inside the last decade and yet there are still industry analysts talking about low-cost locations. I don't think there is much energy left in this idea of promoting regions anyway. Executives sign contracts with other companies, not a region. The best strategy for the CEE IT experts is to spread their delivery across several countries, allowing access to the best expertise in several regions – not just cheap resource in a single location.

IT companies have long talked of partnership, rather than outsourcing. It was often seen as nothing more than a sales message, but take a look at the way that IT services are consumed today and it is clear that executives are making strategic decisions based on the expertise and skills a supplier offers – not their cheap development team.

CHAPTER SEVENTEEN

THE SOFT SKILLS YOU NEED TO WORK IN DEVOPS

DECEMBER 2, 2019

I have written about DevOps recently on this blog. You can look at my DevOps introduction here, but to summarize the concept, DevOps refers to Development Operations.[1] It is a combined set of software development practices that bring together the development of software with IT operations. The aim is to improve the systems development environment so the software lifecycle can be shorter—it's bringing software development closer to the business that it serves.

So far it sounds like DevOps is just focused on software development and the environment used to build software systems—it's all about coding and process. So what are the skills needed to work in DevOps? Logically you might assume that 'hard' subjects such as science, technology, engineering, and mathematics (STEM) might dominate, but I read an article recently that turns this expectation upside down.

Tech Beacon magazine listed four key 'soft' skills that everyone working in DevOps requires and none of them are focused on STEM skills.[2] They are:

1. Collaboration and Communication
2. Empathy
3. Customer Experience
4. Problem Solving

Why would these be the essential skills and not coding or process design? Well, think for a moment about what I said in the introduction—we are bringing the software development process closer to the business that needs this technology system. So some of the key skills will be focused on that process of getting closer to the sponsoring business people.

Collaboration with people outside the IT team will be essential and the ability to communicate technical problems to non-IT professionals. Empathy implies more listening—especially listening to the people who want the system built for their business. Trying to put yourself in the shoes of the customer so you can improve the customer experience is also an important skill that many people ignore, and the ability to solve problems as they are thrown at you is extremely valuable in any team.

I would argue that these four skills are essential for any DevOps team. If you can find people to join the team with all these skills then it is almost certain they can learn the technical skills you need them to use. If you hire for technical ability only then it will be much harder to create great communicators or problem-solvers through training.

It may seem like the opposite to conventional wisdom, but sometimes the best team members on a technical DevOps team are the least technical.

CHAPTER EIGHTEEN

CLOUD SPENDING

JANUARY 4, 2020

What is the fastest developing area of IT that is taking the biggest chunk of your budget? If you said Cloud Computing then you are right. Spending on cloud systems, both for storage and the use of applications, is soaring. A recent survey indicated that cloud now accounts for a quarter of all IT budgets globally.

That's enormous—a quarter of all IT spending globally?

However, it's not a surprise when you consider how cloud computing is expanding and becoming more important at different levels of the organization. Think about the three main areas where cloud strategies are significant:

1. Infrastructure as a Service (IaaS); offering unlimited storage and computing power by buying what you need, when you need it

2. Platform as a Service (PaaS); offering access to platforms on which you can build new services, such as Windows Azure from Microsoft

3. Software as a Service (SaaS); offering access to tools you can use online and only pay for them as you need them—in contrast to software that needs to be installed and maintained locally in your office or on your computers

As you can see, the cloud-based approach is changing how software is designed and used, how platforms that support other solutions are built, and how the raw computing power and storage itself is managed. All these changes in strategy also affect how the services are paid for—in general companies mostly pay for services only as they are used, not up front by purchasing equipment and office space where it can be used.

But there are two issues that are being raised by this change and that is security and how to manage the various cloud systems a large company might be using.

Cloud security is often featured in the news.[1] When we read reports about millions of customers losing their personal data because a company did not secure their cloud then it's a concern. This can be even more important in markets like Europe because of legislation such as GDPR that has the power to heavily fine companies that do not secure customer data.[2]

And all these clouds need some kind of central control—a cloud management platform.[3] There are many (CMP) systems out there and each has a different area of focus—which is the right one for your business and will it be flexible enough to change as your business changes?

These are important areas of business strategy that need to be better controlled and defined for the cloud era. If we are already seeing 25% of the IT budget spent on the cloud and yet there are still concerns over security and CMPs then I'm sure there will be some more cloud disasters before long. A cloud strategy is becoming essential, but make sure that as you design your strategy you also take time to think about and plan how to manage these more difficult issues.

CHAPTER NINETEEN

CAN RPA BREAK FREE OF THE HYPE CYCLE?

JANUARY 20, 2020

Robotic Process Automation (RPA) is one of the hottest areas in the technology industry right now, so why would one of the biggest RPA specialists, UiPath, be laying people off rather than hiring as fast as they can? This was the surprise news last month when UiPath fired 400 employees (from a total of about 3,200) even when the company was valued at over $7 billion after a recent healthy funding round.[1]

UiPath has defended the cuts by saying that they were all strategic. A comment in VentureBeat points out that there are over 90 open jobs at UiPath right now and these cuts really just reflect the end of a period of manic growth–it's time to step back and ensure that everyone is focused on strategic growth.[2]

Speaking to Information Age, Phil Fersht, founder and CEO at HFS Research, said: "UiPath is realizing to its cost that intelligent automation is a marathon, not a sprint. It pushed the hype around RPA far too aggressively."[3]

There are many opinions swirling around, but as these commentators suggest, growth in RPA has been extremely fast. There are many different suppliers all competing in the same market and it's simply not feasible to have over 20 software companies all offering the same—or a very similar service.[4]

It's easy to see why RPA has been hyped by the media and the software companies supplying RPA systems. There is a huge growth in interest in this technology and there are a large number of suppliers all competing for market share. The first to grab a large proportion of market share is most likely to succeed.

I remember visiting IBA Group at the end of last year and talking to their RPA team about how to choose between the various software suppliers. In an ideal world a client would engage a partner like IBA to implement an RPA project and the initial phase would be to evaluate which software would offer the best solution for the specific needs of that company.[5]

Most of the time this structured approach did not appear to be possible because the software companies would rush in, build a pilot to demonstrate their capabilities, and the client would say 'I like that' and ask their technology partner to implement it. Clearly this is not ideal, even with mature technologies, let alone nascent ones that are evolving this rapidly.

There are enough case studies out there now to prove that RPA is not just hype, but it has been in the interest of the leading software companies to ensure it is hyped—excitement is good for business. However, as UiPath has found out, if you are constantly sprinting then you will eventually need to take a rest before continuing with the race.

I am sure that UiPath is going to be OK. They just needed to focus on their product a bit more—manic growth is what happens in every unicorn. The RPA market in general will also be OK–it's proven and there are global case studies that demonstrate the value. Where we will see some change in the months ahead is in more measured thinking and reporting about the value of RPA–it's time to end the hype and really just focus on the benefits. There is already enough to say without the hype anyway.

CHAPTER TWENTY

WHERE WILL CLOUD COMPUTING GO IN 2020?

FEBRUARY 4, 2020

Forrester Research recently published a new research paper exploring how Cloud Computing will change and evolve in 2020.[1] The public cloud market is expected to reach around $411 billion by 2022 so it pays for executives to be thinking ahead to the trends that will shape the market next year.

The research identified 5 key areas to watch:

1. **Change in the player landscape;** large companies such as IBM and Oracle are likely to focus more on applications and development–withdrawing somewhat from cloud services. Alibaba will join AWS, Microsoft, and Google as a leading supplier of cloud services.

2. **SaaS vendors scrapping proprietary platforms;** SaaS vendors need to focus on the applications they are offering, not the basic infrastructure of the cloud. It's likely that

more vendors will just use services such as CloudSuite on AWS.

3. **High Performance Computing in the Cloud;** HPC is expected to increase by at least 40% in 2020. It has traditionally been quite difficult to dynamically allocate (and reduce) resource fast enough to support HPC, but cloud management systems are now getting smart enough for it to be feasible.

4. **Service meshes;** applications are being broken down into smaller and smaller components and these micro service groups are being managed using containers–managing many thousands of these simultaneously is a challenge.

5. **Cloud management focusing on security;** security has always been on the radar for all the cloud management systems, but after the Capital One data breach–which was based on AWS–everyone is now paying far more attention to securing systems and data.

The Forrester research identifies some important trends, not least the creation of a 'Big 4' in cloud services. Alibaba is already a major player in China, but it will be interesting to see if they can develop their services in markets such as Europe and the US.

To my mind the rise in HPC and focus on security are the two important areas to watch. It is becoming possible to do much more with cloud services than ever before and this will lead to more investment and growth, but as more sensitive data and services move to the cloud it will be important to maintain a focus on security–this is one trend that nobody can ignore.

CHAPTER TWENTY ONE

CAN MICROSOFT TAKE THE LEAD IN RPA?

MARCH 10, 2020

The use of Robotic Process Automation (RPA) has exploded in recent years and although some analysts called much of this growth hype there have been many examples and case studies that show the RPA market really is developing fast. One of the most conservative commentators–Hfs Research–even noted that growth last year exceeded their own estimates so this growth is real.[1]

More recent estimates looking to the next few years have stated that we can expect to see market growth of just over 20% each year out to 2025. QY Research notes[2] that there are some specific trends developing in the near future too:

- Due to high technology development and the involvement of developed countries, North America accounts for the largest share in the market for robotic process automation.
- Europe is one of the leading players on the robotic process automation market. Countries like the U.K., Germany and Italy, due to the

> rich manufacturing and automotive industry are the major contributors to market growth.
> - Asia-Pacific is expected to emerge during the forecast period as the fastest growing market. Development of Asian countries and demand for consumer electronic goods compels manufacturers to implement in the manufacturing process a cost-effective technology.

But there is one big RPA story that I have not seen covered by many of the analysts and that is that there is a big new player in town—Microsoft.[3] At present there are over 20 commercial RPA providers around and the top 5 or 6 of them are scooping up most projects, but will Microsoft change the dynamic of which software companies are using?

VentureBeat published a very interesting analysis of the Microsoft plans and they believe it goes far beyond just RPA alone. RPA is starting to define how companies design the software they use (it's more like a platform) so any company offering RPA solutions has the opportunity to also design other solutions too.

However, on the downside the Power Automate system from Microsoft does not yet have as many features as the existing leading RPA software suppliers. Naturally they will work hard to catch up, but at the same time the leaders can keep improving and adding even more features.

Microsoft is coming from behind on RPA as the market is already quite well established. Many will also want to see them update their software, to move through a few versions before trusting it. For these reasons I think that there is potential for change in the RPA market, but if it happens it will be a couple of years from now. In 2020 it will be the existing important players that keep leading.[4]

CHAPTER TWENTY TWO

DIGITAL TWINS ARE MORE THAN JUST 3D MODELS

MARCH 12, 2020

I saw an interesting article[1] describing some of the events at the Geo Buiz Summit[2] in Monterey, California recently. The summit is focused on geospatial innovation so there are many different areas that were covered, but one that caught my eye was on Digital Twins and how we need to move beyond visualization alone if we are to really benefit from this technology.

I have written about Digital Twins[3] in the past. It's a digital replica of a physical entity—living or not. Often the twin represents an engine or a building, a complex environment where sensors are constantly updating the virtual twin so it is as exact a copy as is possible. Airliner engines can be constantly monitored through their twin and real estate can be monitored and controlled without the need for a physical presence.

It is estimated that we will have over 25 billion connected digital sensors by next year so we are certainly going to be seeing more digital twins in use globally. The MIT Sloan Management Review even claimed that we can expect a wave of innovation[4] because many complex systems can be experimented on in a way that would be impossible in the real world– or just too expensive or dangerous.

It is true that when systems can constantly evaluate and diagnose faults we should expect better products and services, but also improvements and innovation. The auto industry is a good example where it is becoming increasingly common for the auto manufacturers to maintain a direct connection with customers after a sale–because the car is constantly feeding data on use and performance back to the manufacturer.

But the Geo Buiz conference topic was interesting because it is usually the 3D model that most people see when looking at a digital twin–the images of an engine or building that can be manipulated on screen. Alexandre Pestov, CEO and Co-founder of vGIS said: "For us, a digital twin is not just a model. For us, a digital twin as an ecosystem where multiple technologies that come together to feed that real-time information, so you can know where things are and how to perform."

That's what I think is really interesting and worth remembering. A digital twin is more than just a 3D model on a computer screen. It is a combination of the Internet of Things (IoT) enabling sensors to constantly provide data, it is the 3D model that renders this information in a visual way allowing changes to be quickly understood, and there is also the living information–for instance in a building, how many people are using it, how many are there now, what is the temperature, etc?

The past five years has seen a clear growth in the interest in Digital Twins and their capabilities.[5] I strongly believe that as we see 5G networks roll out and the IoT become more pervasive, we will see many more examples of how this technology can drive innovation in new ways.

CHAPTER TWENTY THREE

BECOMING STRATEGIC WITH RPA: HOW MANAGERS ARE MISSING THE VALUE ARGUMENT

MARCH 16, 2020

As I have often commented on this blog, many critics of Robotic Process Automation (RPA) have spent years telling the world that it's all hype. One of the actual reasons for this is that many of the benefits of automation are hard to quantify using traditional cost/benefit analysis studies. Given the amount now invested in RPA it is no longer possible to call it a hyped technology, but how are managers measuring the value of these projects?

Managers always take time before launching new projects to plan the Return On Investment (ROI) of any new investment—this is a basic requirement for any new spending—but a new book argues that most managers are not pricing the advantages of RPA correctly.

Yes, it's a book. **Leslie Willcocks, John Hindle and Mary Lacity** are co–authors of 'Becoming Strategic With Robotic Process Automation', published just over a month ago.[1] It is coming from the academic and business school side of this argument–that managers are introducing new technologies into the workplace, but still measuring ROI using old tools and assumptions.

More enlightened managers have started focusing on the Total Cost of Ownership (TCO) when investing in new projects or technologies. However, the authors advise that although this is a step in the right direction, it is still hard to capture the benefit of automation using this model so they have built their own and called it Total Value of Ownership (TVO).

The book argues that to date it has been hard to establish and state all the key benefits of RPA installations therefore this TVO model is required. In traditional business cases only the hard financial costs and benefits are included, but RPA is a strategic tool and therefore the value it creates needs to also be captured. Managers need to understand that RPA is more like a platform on which other solutions can then be created–it is not a tool with a single use and single easily measurable value.

Describing the ideas around TVO, the authors say: "The idea here is to establish every major activity and monitor the five resource costs associated with each activity, across the RPA life-cycle. An understanding of full costs will guide investment strategically, and galvanize commitment to gain substantial returns from the investment. For example, if managers knew the real initial cost of getting the data into shape for use by cognitive tools, they would become much more committed to driving out value from tool adoption."

In their paper on **"Notes From The AI Frontier" (2018),** the McKinsey Global Institute (2018) supports this assumption around value. MGI suggests that by 2030 augmentation and substitution impacts of AI technologies will give a 14% boost beyond 2018 economic performance. But the boost from the impact of AI technologies on product and service innovation and extension will be 24%. Three examples they give are expanding the firm portfolio, increasing channels, and developing new business models. In terms of global GDP. McKinsey estimate the innovation impact of AI technologies as potentially a 7% increase, representing $US six trillion, between 2018 and 2030.

I have yet to read the complete book, but the approach sounds fascinating. What the authors are really suggesting is that we should forget about RPA as an individual tool and stop trying to measure hard and direct benefits–the real value will be in how it completely changes what your company can do a decade from now. It seems to me that a similar argument about productivity could have been made thirty years ago when companies started using email. If managers were doing a cost benefit analysis comparing the cost of sending a letter and sending an email they really were missing the point. That's where we are with RPA today.

Leslie Willcocks, John Hindle and Mary Lacity are co–authors of 'Becoming Strategic With Robotic Process Automation, published in October 2019 and available at **www.sbpublishing.org**. For supporting videos and papers go to **www.roboticandcognitiveautomation.com**

CHAPTER TWENTY FOUR

IOT USE WILL TRIPLE BY 2022– WHAT'S CHANGING?

APRIL 13, 2020

The Internet of Things (IoT) has been hyped for many years. A recent McKinsey report suggests that it has been talked about for at least 15 years, although that sounds a little early to me as many people were only just installing wi-fi networks 15 years ago.[1]

The McKinsey report suggests that the number of companies using the IoT has increased from about 13% in 2014 to about 25% (in late 2019). The projected number of IoT-connected devices is 43 billion by 2023– that's about three times the number we saw in 2018.

Sensor technology is getting cheaper and more advanced as future investments in the sector continue. In fact McKinsey estimates that investment will continue to grow by at least 13.6% until 2022.

Early adopters are now delivering projects at scale and over 200 different types of corporate use have already been documented. We are seeing rapid developments in smart cities, smart cars, connected cars, and e-health. B2B companies selling products to other companies—such as machinery—are able to maintain a constant connection to their equipment now using IoT sensors and Digital Twin software. Most of this would have seemed impossible just 5 years ago.

McKinsey suggests that most of this IoT growth will remain inside the enterprise, although devices that are IoT-connected will see a fast uptake. This sounds correct and I can see IoT devices all around my own home now that were simply not available until recently.

One example is my Amazon Blink system.[2] This system allows easy-to-install security cameras to be placed anywhere. The cameras are controlled by a central module that connects to a phone app, so it's easy to video anything that moves when you are out, or to just check on a live camera feed. Similarly, I have a Furbo camera.[3] This tell me when my dog is barking, allows me to see him, speak to him, and then even to throw a snack to him—all from a phone app.

Many of these applications may seem frivolous, but the important thing to note is that device connectivity is becoming ubiquitous. New cars are now almost all self-diagnosing problems and remaining connected to the manufacturer, constantly passing information on performance back to be checked.

The ongoing rollout of 5G will certainly facilitate an even wider use of sensors on just about everything. 4G develops connectivity issues when many sensors are close together, just like trying to use your phone at a rock concert when you are in a single place with 80,000 other people. As 5G frees us from this problem there will be many new applications, such as a blend of smart cities and smart cars—the vehicles and street furniture transmitting data in both directions.

We are already seeing immense growth in devices and applications that use the IoT, but I believe that 2020 and 2021 will really be the tipping point. Once 5G is more widely available the sky really is the limit–sensors will literally be all around.

CHAPTER TWENTY FIVE

IDC SUGGESTS A FOCUS ON BIG DATA AND AI

APRIL 29, 2020

Research company IDC has issued new guidance on IT spending in 2020. IDC suggests that global spending will be around 3% down on 2019, however there are several areas of interest such as Artificial Intelligence (AI) and Big Data that will see an increase.

In general the approach is that companies need to think strategically about how they will emerge from this challenging year. Digital Transformation and other major projects that might usually take several years to plan and implement are being approved and this is creating opportunities for companies with expertise in these areas.

I believe that we are going to see a wave of transformation this year that positions AI, machine learning, and Big Data analytics at the heart of how many companies are structured. Microsoft is a good example. They rebranded Office 365 to Microsoft 365 and added many new AI capabilities. It's clear that technology companies see the future as an intelligent cloud.

Some companies realized the developing importance of Big Data and the tools required to analyze it some time ago. Alibaba in China is a good example.[1] Originally a retailer the company first started using Big Data analysis to better understand their customers–after all if you get to the point where you can almost predict what a customer needs then you can dramatically improve the customer experience and also drive more sales.

Today, Alibaba offers a much wider range of services and this has largely been driven by their experience and expertise using Big Data. As the wave of transformation projects grows large in 2020 it will be the ability of brands to gather and analyze data that makes all the difference.

Conversely, gathering all this data requires planning and permission. Tools such as facial recognition have faced problems because of concerns over customer privacy, but these tools have found many new applications. A good example is the Brazilian car sharing company, Turbi.[2] They allows customers to unlock a car based on facial recognition–it beats the usual tedious procedures required when renting a car.

Where these tools improve the life of end customers, they will be accepted and popular. Now brands must explore how they can use AI and Big Data to transform the service they are offering. These tools allow behavioral insight in real time.

It's easy to imagine how important this could be for a wide variety of companies. Retailers can predict when customers will shop and what they will want. Telcos can flexibly offer different service packages to customers based on data use. Banks can reduce the need for collections by intervening early with customers who may be about to default.

Although IDC suggests that IT spending will be reduced this year, it will increase in these specific areas. Companies are looking to evolve into 2021 with a new approach and, for some, this will be a dramatic change. 2020 is the year of Big Data.

CHAPTER TWENTY SIX

WHY IS THERE IS A GLOBAL BOOM FOR MAINFRAMES AND COBOL?

MAY 12, 2020

Mainframes are hot in 2020.[1] I never thought I would write that sentence, but the Covid-19 coronavirus pandemic has led to a situation where many industries using mainframes need to change their business model, or operating structure, with an agility they are just not used to. Mainframe expertise is needed–and fast.

A good example is government systems, especially social security or unemployment benefits. New rules have been drafted almost overnight by some governments. Systems and processes that usually take months to plan and implement have been changed overnight.

When the US government passed the CARES Act[2] and suddenly million of people expected help to be wired to their bank account–or to receive a physical check in the post–the biggest problem was reworking the mainframe systems that support all these processes.

When I studied software engineering in the late eighties and early nineties I had to study the difference between mainframe systems and the IBM PCs taking over the world at that time. We did use a Prime mainframe[3], but even 30 years ago, many of us felt that the mainframe was a dinosaur because computing power was rapidly coming to every desk. I was even carrying an early Cambridge laptop[4] back then so that made the mainframe look even more archaic.

You might think that this attitude to mainframes should be even more true today, because we all carry around more computing power in our phones than NASA had back when they put a man on the moon.[5] But across the world mainframes are still out there processing data for airlines, government agencies and highly regulated industries, such as banks, where rapid change is difficult.

Computer science students today don't really focus on mainframes. Students want to build mobile apps, games, or code for computers that are widely used. I tried using Google earlier today to find a computer science course that included mainframes and I couldn't find any—if they do exist then they are well hidden.

This means that there is a scarcity of resource for maintenance and improvement—especially the emergency changes that airlines and governments need. There is a need to create a more agile system of managing mainframe maintenance. If companies are going to rely on mainframes in future then they need to build a more resilient system that allows change and control over their processes.

A related problem is that much of the business software developed to help airlines manage ticket sales or banks process transactions was written in COBOL— which means Common Business Oriented Language.[6]

It's a computer language that rose in popularity along with mainframes—and then declined as the mainframes also declined.

So we are in a situation where it is hard to find people who can maintain the machines, but it is also hard to find people who can change the software too. Most software developers with COBOL experience have retired—it is no longer commonly studied in university.

The Covid-19 coronavirus pandemic has vividly demonstrated why we need mainframe and COBOL expertise—many government systems cannot be easily changed without this knowledge and expertise. In Oklahoma it is taking over 2 weeks to process unemployment claims. Newly unemployed citizens have a right to these extra benefits during the crisis and yet because the mainframe systems are so slow and cumbersome—and COBOL programmers are so scarce—people are not being helped.

The last time Gartner counted COBOL experts in the USA was 2004.[7] They counted 2 million back then, but also noted that each year 5% of those experts retire. My math may not be great, but that means they are now almost all retired.

There are mainframes out there delivering critical infrastructure and they are using billions of lines of COBOL code that very few people now understand. The problem is made worse because anyone who studies COBOL today would find themselves focusing on maintenance work—it's not as inspiring as launching a new app.

This reliance on mainframes and COBOL has been highlighted by the pandemic. These systems need to be managed more effectively.

This is exactly where companies like IBA Group may be able to step in. In the CEE region there are many mainframe and COBOL experts still working and many have applied modern DevOps processes to the management of mainframes.[8] Not only do they still have the skills available, they have created improved systems for automated and management.

CHAPTER TWENTY SEVEN

DEVOPS HAS REDEFINED HOW TO MANAGE MAINFRAME SYSTEMS

JUNE 12, 2020

My first job after I studied software engineering at college was software development.[1] I was hired by the German technology company Siemens Nixdorf[2] to write electronic-point-of-sale software for several British retail brands, including Tesco and Dixons.[3] In the 90s, if you shopped at Tesco then it was my code checking if your credit card was valid.

Back then, there was really no concept of DevOps.[4] I'd plan my code, write it, compile it, and then check it works on a test system. Even the testing was not all that comprehensive. I had some test scripts that helped to ensure I had not fixed one problem and created another, but it was not 100% bulletproof. Once I felt that it all looked OK I could transfer the code into production.

With modern DevOps the development and operation, or support, of the system is more holistic. It brings together the coding process with the process of managing the entire system rather than just the coder being able to throw their new code over a big wall and then run away because it is no longer their problem.

DevOps really originated from Agile software development methodologies.[5] When I was coding the retail systems we were still using the waterfall development method, but later in my coding career I was managing software development for a bank and using Agile–so I have seen this up close.[6] The difference is enormous. With Agile you make small changes, but often, and also have a way to revert back to the current system if anything goes wrong. It's an incremental approach that continually improves the system, rather than just doing an enormous update twice a year.

I recently recorded a video with IBA Group[7] where I talked to one of their DevOps engineers, Yuliya Varonina[8], about the changing nature of mainframe development and how DevOps is now an integral component of modern mainframe management. This was a really interesting insight for me because I personally last used a mainframe when I was back at college (a Prime[9]), despite having a career focused on using IT or writing about it.

My expectation was that the importance of mainframes has sharply declined in recent years, but the coronavirus pandemic reminded everyone that there are banks, airlines, and government departments[10] still relying on these systems and companies such as IBM are continuing to launch[11] new mainframes with enormous computing power. The mainframe never went away even though most people working in IT started focusing on other platforms.

Airlines forced to issue a huge number of refunds as schedules were revised needed to quickly change their systems. Banks needed to find a way to process millions of unusual payments as governments issued stimulus payments and government departments–especially health agencies–were overrun with requests for help. Everyone needed the ability to quickly modify how their mainframe systems worked and in some cases it was extremely difficult. Many Americans found that they couldn't claim any stimulus payments because they needed to register as unemployed and the system was flooded with too many requests–the system itself was poorly managed and completely unstructured.[12]

This pandemic has reminded many executives that their companies rely on mainframes and those mainframes need to be managed in a structured way.[13] They need modern DevOps so code changes can easily be tested and applied to production without huge delays. Even if you have never previously understood or thought about how DevOps could improve the management of your mainframe systems, it is now essential.

I'd recommend watching the conversation I had with Yuliya because she explains in a clear and enthusiastic manner how important it is to modernize the management of mainframes. Follow this reference to watch the 11-minute video now.[14]

CHAPTER TWENTY EIGHT

DATA SCIENCE IS THE NEW ROCK & ROLL

JULY 7, 2020

Every now and then there is a particular skill or discipline that just suddenly becomes important, especially in the IT industry. In recent years app developers suddenly found they were hugely in demand and before that it was coders who could quickly create interactive websites. Now it's happening in data science.[1]

As an academic discipline data science has existed for decades. Many universities have long-established departments that may have been running alongside the mathematics or statistics departments since the 60s or 70s.

But data science is developing a new importance in the business environment of 2020 because data mining, big data, unstructured data, and machine learning are all becoming important tools for modern companies struggling to handle vast quantities of data.

We are creating more data than ever before. The World Economic Forum has estimated[2] that by 2025 we will be creating 463 exabytes of new data daily–that's about 212 million new DVDs everyday. IBM has estimated_that 90% of all the data that exists was created in just the past two years—and that is growing exponentially.[3]

In 2019, 2.9 million data science job openings were created—this will certainly increase in 2020.[4] According to the US Bureau of Labor Statistics, 11.5 million new jobs in data science will be created by the year 2026—that's just in the US. It is safe to say that if you want a secure future over the next few years then studying data science will help.

There are many applications for data science across many industries, but just to illustrate how wide-ranging the application of this technology really is think about some of these examples:

- Agriculture: machine learning and artificial intelligence (AI) will increasingly help with pricing, forecasting, and improving farm output.
- Healthcare: companies like IBM already have oncology diagnostic systems. The application of AI in further health diagnostic systems will be a huge growth area.
- Aviation: improving flight schedules, customer experience, planning maintenance are all area where airlines can use improved insights into the data they have.
- Cyber Security: the ability to spot unusual activity inside a company by constantly analyzing data on the network activity of all employees and customers
- Customer Experience: being able to predict the behavior of customers will be an important attribute for many different companies. Banks can predict customers who may default and

retailers can predict what customers may want to buy.

Data science is changing how companies are organized. Many are stating that they see an ability to use AI as their future. So it's a great place to seek a job, but if you are working in a company that has yet to explore the benefits of data science then it might be time to start thinking about an expert partner—before it's too late.

CHAPTER TWENTY NINE

MODERNIZING THE MAINFRAME: OPEN SOURCE TRENDS

JULY 10, 2020

Earlier in my career, I managed an international technology team for a major bank.[1] We developed and supported all the equity trading systems used by the bank, so it was a global operation, connecting our systems to all the major stock exchanges around the world.

We started moving some of our servers over to Linux because it seemed to be easier to support than Windows servers. It was never really a question of cost, because the real cost with a server farm was maintaining it, rather than the cost of a software license.

But at the time it was quite difficult to convince my managers that a critical part of the bank infrastructure could run on open source systems–free software created by a global development community–rather than a private company like Microsoft.

Eventually we tried a pilot and it worked so well that we went much further than originally planned. I was thinking back to this experience when I had a conversation with Sergey Beganski[2], the head of the mainframe department focused on new technologies at IBA Group.[3]

Sergey outlined some of the advantages of using open source systems, and they matched up with my own experience. He said: "People are interested in open source because it gives them value. Some say it is free. I would say it is cost-effective. If you or your company are active in the open source community, you earn a good reputation. It is also very easy to adjust open source software to your needs because any developer can make changes in the code and add the required functionality."

It was reassuring to hear that Sergey's arguments were similar to my own, back in my banking days. One of the reasons I struggled to get my boss to listen to me was because there was a concern about the security and reliability of "free" software. I asked Sergey how he manages this in 2020.

He said: "Open source code can be even higher quality than traditional code because it is not just a team of a few developers who work on it, but thousands of developers from around the world. All of them have unique experience in different technologies, industries, and projects. With more eyes on the code, they find and fix the bugs very quickly."

On the specific question about security Sergey added: "Open source software has strong protection. The open source community finds security holes quickly. They notify the code owner about bugs, and the owner fixes them immediately."

I was not aware of a big open source movement in mainframe systems until the team at IBA Group informed me that there is a trend in this area, so I asked Sergey which companies or organizations are leading this. He explained: "Open source for mainframes has not become widespread yet, but recently some important players like IBM, Broadcom, and Rocket made a decision to use this approach to software development."

He added: "They launched the Open Mainframe Project[4] within the Linux Foundation[5] to implement open source projects for the mainframe. Currently, the biggest project of the Linux Foundation is ZOWE.[6] This new open source software platform enables developers to use modern tools and technologies for mainframe systems on z/OS."

There are many examples[7] of organizations that struggle to support mainframe systems, especially because they cannot find enough skilled resource. I asked Sergey if a focus on open source can help with this problem.

He said: "It is no secret that one of the key problems with mainframes is that the cohort of programmers supporting them has been shrinking. Projects like ZOWE attract the younger generation to the mainframe platform and make it more popular and understandable for developers."

That's good news for the entire mainframe community. I asked Sergey if he has any examples of projects or pilots that he has worked on recently. He said: "I am really interested in the development of open source for the mainframe. Our teams have developed custom software for our clients using the ZOWE framework and have delivered some pilots already.

Sergey added: "For example, we developed a plugin for the Visual Studio Code using the ZOWE framework to convert Assembler to C. And one of our custom projects involves the development of a web interface using the ZOWE Framework."

The development of open source inside the mainframe community is a very interesting trend that appears to be developing quickly. This conversation with Sergey gave me some great insights into just how far open source has changed and evolved.

CHAPTER THIRTY

SEEK QUICK WINS WITH HIGH IMPACT IF YOU WANT DATA ANALYTICS TO SUCCEED

JULY 29, 2020

The Harvard Business Review (HBR)[1] is well-known for their leading research, presented in a format that is easy to digest. I was therefore pleased to see that they recently published a guide to data analytics and the five different approaches that most companies take when they build out a data science strategy.[2] What's really interesting about the article is that of the five common approaches, two almost always fail, two work partially, and one actually works. Here is a short summary of the different approaches outlined in the HBR:

1. **What problems do you need to solve?** This is generally when the CEO hires a data scientist or sets up a team and they go off looking for problems to solve with data, but without any specific guidance from the business.

2. **Boil the ocean.** Spending millions and trying to change the entire business without first fixing

all the legacy data issues inside the company, therefore having almost no impact.

3. **Let a thousand flowers bloom.** Embracing data analytics from the top level and encouraging each business unit to use it, but not forcing or guiding them on what they can achieve.

4. **Three years and $10m from now it will be great.** Building out committees and workshops and designing change that may only take effect years in the future can possibly work, but often it will not. People lose interest and move on.

5. **Start with high-leverage business problems.** To build value quickly, identify the quick wins where data analytics can have a direct impact on the business and seek these opportunities across every team.

As you might expect, it's the first two that don't work, the next two that can work sometimes, and the final approach that works best. It works because it is pragmatic. First you identify some projects that could really benefit from using data analytics and promote the impact that it has had on these areas. Other teams will naturally want to learn from the initial data analytics projects and will take it further.

This pragmatic approach and focus on quick wins is frequently used by consultants advising on major change programs so it is a surprise that with data analytics it is not often applied. I believe this is because there are so many fascinating use cases for data analytics that it looks like a done deal–it has to be good for the business so there is no need to run pilots or seek quick wins.

This is a dangerous approach for any business and reminds me of when CEOs rushed to buy expensive CRM systems without building any of the processes and people training they would need to make it work. Technology itself, including data analytics, is never a quick fix. You need to identify specific areas of the business where it could make the quickest impact and then communicate the results so people across the business buy into the new ideas and systems.

CHAPTER THIRTY ONE

MODERNIZING THE MAINFRAME: OPEN SOURCE SUMMIT AND TRENDS

NOVEMBER 5, 2020

The Linux Foundation just hosted[1] their first ever virtual summit. It was forced online by the Covid-19 pandemic, but proved to be an extremely immersive experience that attracted over 4,000 participants from 109 different countries.

This event was facilitated by the online platform InXpo.[2] This platform allows conference organizers to gamify the entire experience of attending a virtual event—hundreds of sessions and tutorials can be scheduled alongside virtual sponsor showcases and booths.

I think that it's very interesting to see how events are being virtualized in a more sophisticated way than the earlier attempts to just stream a keynote speech. Conferences like this one hosted by the Linux Foundation are genuinely developing a way to be immersive and inclusive without requiring travel to a conference location.

The success of this event just demonstrates the continued interest across the world in open source software and systems. Google has recently launched the Open Usage Commons[3] to address some of the problems that open source developers have been having with projects in recent years. In particular, once a product or system is developed and released into the world it can be difficult to keep track of the product name and versions, because open source code is open and available to anyone. The Google system allows products to be trademarked and then openly shared, but in a more controlled way.

There is now a significant 'bootstrapping' community[4] amongst corporate IT leadership. These are IT executives and decision-markers actively looking for open source solutions and products to come bubbling up in their business area. They actively try to support and promote interesting new products, helping to create a critical mass of developers all contributing to a project.

All this is a world away from when I was managing a global software development team two decades ago and it was a controversial decision to migrate to Linux servers for our critical systems and infrastructure. Eventually my company had a very positive experience of building out an open source server farm and they expanded on that dramatically.

Now we can see that open source standards have been extended beyond systems such as servers and even into mainframes. At The Open Source Summit I mentioned earlier there was a big announcement by the Open Mainframe Project[5] about the long-term support for Zowe[6]–the open source integration platform for mainframes running IBM's z/OS. The Zowe framework is part of a broader initiative to make z/OS more accessible.

Rather than requiring IT teams to acquire and retain specialized skills, IBM and other independent software vendors in the mainframe ecosystem, have been modernizing tools and processes as part of an effort to make mainframes running z/OS function more like any other platform an IT organization may deploy.

Announcements like this renewed support for Zowe reinforce how important communities (such as mainframe developers) are becoming for the wider open source movement. With major industry giants like Google now lining up to help facilitate more open source projects and corporate leaders bootstrapping great new ideas the entire open source community is not just becoming normalized, it is being championed.

I fully expect to see many new corporate tools, using a variety of platforms, launched in the new few years completely based on open source development. Many will be cloud-based systems that can be accessed and paid for when needed, but the open source approach is also shaking up other areas, such as mainframes. This is an important area to follow because, as the announcements at the recent Open Source Summit demonstrate, change is coming fast and major brands such as IBM and Google, are helping the wider industry to focus on where open source can be more widely used.

I recently had a conversation with Sergey Beganski[7], the head of the mainframe department focused on new technologies at IBA Group.[8] We focused on mainframes and open source and you can view the video conversation by clicking here.[9]

CHAPTER THIRTY TWO

GARTNER STRATEGIC PREDICTIONS FOR 2021: SEISMIC CHANGE COMING SOON

DECEMBER 16, 2020

The analyst firm Gartner has just released their Top Ten Strategic Predictions for 2021 and Beyond.[1] It's often a repetitive trope every November and December to see analysts making predictions for the year ahead, but 2020 has been a year like no other. The only comparable pandemic to Covid-19 was the Spanish Flu and that was a century ago.

There are so many questions for business leaders at present. How they might need to accelerate digital transformation to stay relevant in the 'new normal.' How they might need to embrace distributed working so some workers can stay at home boosting resilience for the organization. How technologies can be used to create safer working environments. What will happen first?

I'm selecting a few of the Gartner ideas and predictions here, especially those that are more likely to affect the day-to-day operation of most organizations in the short-term. The first trend of importance to my mind is the elevation of the CIO. Gartner suggests that by 2024 a quarter of all large enterprise CIOs will be responsible for operational results because digital acceleration will redefine the organization–therefore the CIO effectively will become the COO.

Some of the other expected changes include:

- **At leads 75% of all conversations at work being recorded.** The aim being to monitor employee experience and satisfaction and drilling into conversations to generate new ideas. I have long suspected that this may be an effect of the work-from-home trend and it's not (always) as invasive as it sounds. I believe the first wave will be to ensure that all meetings and decisions are recorded and made available to everyone, to encourage more transparency in the organization, even with many people outside the office. Handled well, this could be a positive change.

- **GigCX explosion.** Gartner suggests that by 2025 around 75% of all customer questions will be handled by a freelance customer service expert. We are moving away from the age of the low-paid contact center agent and into the world of freelance experts using cloud-based virtual platforms to be connected to customers.

- **Content moderation is essential.** At present, we tend to think of content moderation as a process that social media companies use to ensure that their sites are not flooded with pornography or terrorism-related content. Gartner is suggesting that by 2024, content moderation will be an essential process for over 30% of all organizations. If you have any kind of online presence then the management of polarizing content will be essential.

- **Farms and factories are automated:** this is automation on a grand scale. Gartner suggests that by 2025 the customer will be the first human to touch over 20% of all products we purchase—both food and consumer products.

Many of these changes were in play already. Even before the Covid-19 pandemic there was a push for automation, but now there is an accelerated demand for change. Many companies that were previously just interested in using the Internet of Things (IoT) and digital twins are now pushing ahead with those projects faster than planned because smarter maintenance guided by automated sensors helps to keep employees safer.

Some of these more dramatic changes, like most meetings being recorded, are being driven by the need to restructure how organizations function. A distributed workplace is very different to just seeing everyone work together inside a hub. meetings, interactions, and especially decisions, need to be approached differently and it will be a combination of technology platforms and new processes that facilitate this evolution.

The underlying theme of the Gartner Strategic Predictions for 2021 is that the organization itself is about to change quite dramatically. This may be a painful experience for those used to wearing a suit and commuting to an office each morning—technology is about to redefine what it means to have a job, how you are contracted to a company, and how organizations function. 2021 is going to be a seismic shift and technology is driving this change.

CHAPTER THIRTY THREE

GARTNER STRATEGIC PREDICTIONS FOR 2021: DIGITAL DISRUPTION IS THE MESSAGE FOR 2021

JANUARY 25, 2021

As I mentioned in my last blog, the analyst firm Gartner has just released[1] their Top Ten Strategic Predictions for 2021 and Beyond. This is an insightful look at some of the key changes that might take place in 2021 and, as you might expect, much of the change is coming from technological innovation.

More specifically, there is an acceleration of digital transformation taking place that was spurred on by the Covid-19 pandemic. In some cases, organizations had to change fast just to survive—retailers that did not have a comprehensive online service for example. In other cases we have seen rapid change because new ways of working are being embraced, such as the majority of employees working from home.

But in an additional note to the strategic predictions, Gartner also published their view on digital disruptions that may take place in the next five years[2] and dramatically impact how businesses operate in the near future. These are fascinating and range from DNA storage to human augmentation. They are describing a world where your Amazon Echo can run a test on your voice to check for dementia–and more importantly, this is all predicted to take place in the near future.

So what are some of the digital disruptions Gartner predicts before 2025, and why should we pay attention? Here are some that I think really stand out:

- **Non-traditional computing:** Moore's Law[3] has served us well for decades now, but it describes the constant evolution of binary computing. Deep neural networks, DNA storage, and quantum computing are expanding the power of computers and this could create enormous new opportunities for organizations. For a simple description of the power of quantum computing listen to Canadian Prime Minister Justin Trudeau[4] answering a reporter–who clearly expected the politician to be unable to answer the question. Areas such as cryptography will be enormously influenced by the increased power becoming available.

- **Global digital twins:** we are seeing organizations using digital twins far more than ever, but what happens when we can start merging data from various sensors to create a digital model of the earth? Can we use it to track climate change, pollution, traffic and plan how to move around cities? What if we could be alerted to fires the moment they start so the enormous wild fires regularly threatening places like California could be controlled more easily?

- **Biohacking:** many people are concerned about the privacy of their private data, especially health data, and yet they publish these views on tools like Facebook–an oxymoron. But with so many IoT sensors now being deployed, almost everything is being tracked and listened to. If a camera in a public park can identify that you have a health problem then the question is not so much how do we maintain privacy, it should be more focused on how our private data is used–it is already being collected, we need to control what happens to it.

- **Greater organizational monitoring:** I mentioned in my last blog that recording conversations will be more common in the organization. I believe it will start with meetings, but Gartner suggested it could possibly be everything said in the workplace. There may also be a dramatic increase in the measure of emotional experiences and engagement. This will determine how people are feeling at work–are they happy and comfortable or anxious? This type of measurement could also be used by advertisers to place ads in front of us depending on our mood, location, and personal preferences.

Some of these disruptions feel far away, as if they might have little impact on the immediate future, but think for a moment about how the next few years will play out. If the hackers are using quantum computing to bypass your security then they may have systems that are thousands of times more powerful than your line of defense.

There is a common theme running through many of these disruptions and this is the way that data is being used—what will remain private and what can organizations use. Is it ethical to check my mood before serving me an ad for a new soft drink? Can an airline really prevent me from boarding a plane if I can't prove that I am vaccinated against Covid-19?

Many of these disruptions around data and privacy are going to dramatically change how organizations do business in the near future—creating some opportunities, but also many challenges. We need to start preparing for the way these disruptions will change consumer behavior and subsequently how companies need to evolve to serve those consumers.

CHAPTER THIRTY FOUR

COVID GIVES A DRAMATIC BOOST TO DIGITAL TWINS

FEBRUARY 4, 2021

I have written in the past about digital twins and the opportunities they offer for companies to create a virtual representation of a real engine, building, or other object.[1] The digital version can be used for experiments or monitoring using sensors–like checking all the fire exits in a building and highlighting if any fire doors have been propped open.

Shell is a good example.[2] The oil and gas giant uses digital twins to model facilities such as oil exploration platforms. The digital twin is used to manage assets and improve safety through actions such as predictive maintenance. Sensors on the platform feed information back to the digital twin and can report on wear and tear– so instead of laborious manual checks, the engineers know exactly where they need to focus attention.

The Covid-19 pandemic has created a strong incentive for companies to explore digital twins in more detail because they can help reduce the number of people needed to maintain facilities. The digital twin allows maintenance to be proactive, rather than reactive–just fixing problems or running periodic checks without any insight.

The industry analyst Gartner published[3] a survey recently that suggested the use of digital twins is growing quickly. 31% of survey respondents said that they use digital twins to improve their employee or customer safety, such as the use of remote asset monitoring to reduce the frequency of in-person monitoring for hospital patients and mining operations, for example. The survey showed that 27% of companies plan to use digital twins as autonomous equipment, robots or vehicles.

The Gartner research suggests that by 2023, one-third of all mid to large-sized companies that have used the Internet of Things (IoT) will have implemented at least one digital twin project that was associated with Covid-19.

There are some interesting connections here. The IoT is being explored in more detail because it offers the opportunity to change how people work. Monitoring sensors can be used far more securely than physically having to go out testing assets. Because of the greater adoption of IoT the use of a digital twin is increasingly attractive.

This is subsequently leading to a wider adoption of Artificial Intelligence (AI) as well. This is so the digital twin can learn about the surrounding area and begin to understand what the sensors are reporting–it is possible to ensure that alarms are only sounded when there is a genuine problem, rather than a temporary change in the data.

Last year Gartner found[4] that only 13% of companies were actively using digital twins, but they observed that 62% were investigating the area and planned to be using a digital twin before the end of 2020. The Covid-19 pandemic has just accelerated this digital transformation. By next year I expect that we will see more than a third of all companies using digital twins for some applications, even if it is just monitoring how the office is being used to ensure employee safety.

I think it's also important to emphasize that digital twins are not being used in isolation. A digital twin strategy requires a focus on how IoT can be used and how AI can generate insights into the data being reported by the sensors. There is a chance for companies to become much smarter—will your organization embrace this opportunity for an AI transformation with a digital twin?

CHAPTER THIRTY FIVE

HOW THE IOT CREATES A NEED FOR DIGITAL TWINS

FEBRUARY 26, 2021

'Digital twins' have been around in engineering for a long time.[1] When an airline buys an engine from a company like Rolls Royce they are not just buying an engine. They will also have ongoing monitoring and maintenance of that engine. Sensors inside the engine will broadcast information to Rolls Royce, who will maintain a completely virtual version of the same engine. Updated in real-time this allows the engine manufacturer to know when maintenance is required and if there are any problems developing.

So engineers have known about digital twins, and the software and sensors needed to manage systems like this, for many years, but it has not become familiar to the general population in the same as as Artificial Intelligence. However, this may change in the near future.

The Internet of Things (IoT) is how we generally describe the emerging environment where every electronic device is identifiable and connected.[2] Everyone can already see this in their home environment. It used to be that the only device connected to the Internet was a computer. Now your phones, Kindles, iPads, cameras, toys, and many other devices will all be connected. The next step is for sensors to be everywhere so you can control lights, temperature, locks on doors etc.

This is already possible, but it requires the homeowner to invest in changing devices that already work–like replacing traditional locks with electronic connected locks. Scaling up to the level of smart cities is where the IoT really creates a requirement for digital twins.

The MIT Sloan Management Review recently published a story detailing how the loss of the Notre Dame Cathedral in Paris to fire was mitigated by the fact that a digital twin had been created by academics interested in preserving ancient structures.[3] By next year, Gartner has estimated that there will be over 25 billion connected sensors all over the world. This has particular importance for city planners–not just because they can rebuild cathedrals lost to fire.

These sensors offer real-time data on how a city is functioning. Traffic, pedestrian flow, weather, air quality, can all be measured and monitored and through the use of the digital twin, a model of the city can display live data or can explore time periods or trends. The ability to diagnose problems in the city–such as potholes in a major road–automatically allows the system to allocate resource to fix problems immediately.

It has become common to model entire buildings using digital twin technology, allowing landlords the ability to monitor and control every aspect of the building from heating to fire safety systems. The increasing realization that this can be scaled up to entire cities, to create a graphical representation of water supply, electricity supply, and other important utilities, is an important development that is being assisted by the increased use of the IoT and the ongoing rollout of 5G telecoms in many countries.

I believe we are about to hit a wave of innovation where 5G facilities a greater rollout of IoT sensors and devices and this in turn leads to the need to be able to capture and control all these sensors in some form of model. The digital twin is about to go mainstream.

CHAPTER THIRTY SIX

WHAT'S THE IMMEDIATE FUTURE FOR CHATBOTS AND VOICE RECOGNITION?

MARCH 9, 2021

Over the next few months I want to focus here on the intersection between technology and business solutions. As someone who initially studied software engineering and also for an MBA focused on organizational psychology, I'm comfortable connecting business needs with technology, but I realize that sometimes the two areas don't meet. Important technological tools or ideas are not supported by business leaders just because they don't understand the value of these ideas.

So let's begin by looking at voice recognition. In the 1960s the classic science-fiction TV show, Star Trek, featured Captain Kirk and his crew talking to a computer.[1] At the time it seemed unbelievable and in the fourth edition of the Star Trek movies the engineer Scotty travels back in time to 1986 and is confused when he has to use a keyboard to work with a computer.[2]

In the present day the idea of talking to a computer has been completely normalized through the popularity of home assistant devices such as the Amazon Echo, Google Home, and Apple's Siri. I can talk to my Chevrolet car and easily send a WhatsApp message using Siri and that's a lot safer (and more legal) than trying to type a message when driving.[3]

But voice interactions are still a bit one-sided. I can ask Alexa to tell me a joke, but I can't ask her to explain why blue contrasts well with yellow or why Monty Python is funny. We can issue commands, but we can't really have a conversation yet.

But researchers around the world are working hard to improve this. Google demonstrated their Assistant almost three years ago and claimed that it could handle natural speech and make decisions on behalf of the user. Their most famous demonstration was asking the assistant to call and make a booking for a haircut.[4] It was impressive, but at the time I was always thinking, what if the hairdresser taking the booking asks anything unexpected? What would Google say?

The reality is that this problem is like an onion. There are layers of complexity. Imagine if the hairdresser responded by saying, there is no parking available on the day you have booked so will you be able to manage to locate parking elsewhere? This is a normal question and yet it would not fit into the normal narrative of booking an appointment. If the Assistant is smart enough then faced with this kind of problem it would say something like, I will inform my client of the situation and we will contact you again if there is a problem.

If the Assistant is completely confused then that's a problem for everyone. It's rather like the customer service chatbots that have become so popular as companies ask us to talk to a robot, rather than a real person in a contact center. It saves the company money if they can automate all these interactions, but when customers have a problem that is outside the range of what the robot understands then it is a painful and frustrating experience.

I recently faced difficulty with PayPal. I was locked out and needed to reset my account, but they wanted to send a reset code to my phone and they had an old phone number that I no longer use. There was no other way to reset my account so I started a conversation with the help system only to find I was talking to a bot. I asked for help updating my phone number, but for that I needed to login. I was stuck in a Kafkaesque loop and the bot didn't understand my frustration. I only managed to get help from a real human when I called out their poor customer service system on Twitter.

The Watson system from IBM is currently one of the most advanced examples of Natural Language Processing (NLP)[5] and Automatic Speech Recognition (ASR)[6] in the world today. IBM has been working on speech recognition systems since 1962, when their original system could understand 16 different words–perhaps they inspired Captain Kirk?

ASR is an extremely useful tool for many companies in several ways. Think about a customer service center. Hundreds of agents are constantly talking to your customers and it's all simultaneous. How do the team leaders and managers ensure quality is kept high and problematic calls are checked? They used to just sample a small percentage of the calls, which means that many will be missed. Now they can apply a system like ASR to all the voice traffic, convert the conversations into text data and then analyze the content and perform sentiment or quality analysis–this can also be very important for compliance in regulated industries.

NLP is where the really exciting work is taking place. The IBM Watson research is taking natural voice recognition and processing to a new level, so the system can understand idioms and sarcasm, names and places, and actually interact seamlessly. Business applications include personal assistants, machine translation, chatbots, sentiment analysis, and even spam detection.

As my PayPal experience shows, I am particularly interested in how tools like Watson can improve that customer to brand interaction and experience. If I could just talk to the brand and explain my problem (and be understood) then it would be a dramatic improvement on the present-day situation where I have to first work out how I can find a human who will listen to my problem. NLP could be a game-changer for many companies and although I think the real human experience will probably remain important in customer service for several years, it seems that more and more basic types of interaction will be handled automatically.

In my lifetime I believe that we will move from commanding Alexa to start playing a David Bowie album to full and rich conversations. Maybe we will not be able to talk about the books of Jean-Paul Sartre, but at least it should be possible to ask DHL where my package is and to receive a sensible answer.

CHAPTER THIRTY SEVEN

HOW CAN COMPANIES BENEFIT FROM MACHINE LEARNING?

MARCH 16, 2021

Machine Learning (ML) is one of those technical subjects that keeps on being mentioned as a business solution. It is often confused with Artificial Intelligence (AI), so it's worth stating here at the start that there is a difference. AI is the simulation of human thought or behavior and ML is the ability to learn and draw conclusions from data without being explicitly programmed to do so–the machine can just look at the data and start drawing conclusions.

The two subjects are often connected because ML can be used as a subset of AI. You build a system that analyzes data and learns from it and this can then trigger the AI to make certain decisions. Connected, but not quite the same.

A good example of machine learning is the ability to learn from images. Type 'dog' into Google image search and you will see millions of photos of dogs, but Google doesn't need to only use images that were labelled as a dog by whoever uploaded it. By training the system they can feed it a large number of images that are verified as dogs and then the system can learn the distinguishing features, allowing it to recognize an image as a dog in future even if it has no further information—in the same way a human can recognize a photo as a dog even if it is a photo we have never seen.

This all sounds a bit complex and mathematical and as you might expect, it is complex. If you follow the ML community online then you can see arguments raging over complex subjects that the rest of the world cannot understand. However, a general understanding of the possibilities of ML are important for business leaders because this is going to create several opportunities in many industries. It is getting easier to deploy these solutions as well. Companies like IBM with their Watson product offer ML solutions in the cloud—you don't need to build anything, just pay as you go.[1]

Every executive knows that their company has a huge amount of data on customers. You know what they purchase, what they like and dislike, and even how they behave on different days of the week. By applying ML to this information it should be possible to accurately predict the behavior of customers and to personalize the experience you give to them. Here are a few more specific ideas[2] of business solutions that can be powered by ML:

1. **Customer lifetime value modeling:** who are your best customers? What differentiates them from others? Are there ways you can nudge good customers so they become great customers? Learning about the behavior of customers over a long period of time can yield incredible insights into how you can serve them better.

2. **Churn modeling:** many subscription businesses rely on customers paying a bill every month—video streaming, Internet, mobile phone contracts. If you can analyze customer behavior and predict which ones plan to leave your service before it happens then that's extremely powerful and can allow you to offer a deal that may retain the customer.

3. **Dynamic pricing:** industries such as airlines and hotels can learn from past behavior to dynamically price their services, rather than only ever using fixed rates. Don't leave cash on the table when your customers are prepared to pay more.

4. **Customer segmentation:** can you categorize your customers using finer granularity, rather than the very broad use of demographics or location? What does it reveal? Can you learn from one group of customers and apply those lessons to others?

5. **Recommendations and special offers:** linked to churn modeling, but not restricted to subscription businesses. If you know your customer always shops at the end of the month and likes a particular category of products then you can help to trigger purchasing activity with highly personalized special offers or recommendations that are targeted at the individual customer.

In the customer service environment there are also many applications for ML to work on predictive support.[3] It's possible to listen to a conversation between a customer and support agent in the contact center and for the system to be presenting the agent with the most likely solution to the customer's problem—before they even need to search for the information. It just pops up automatically.

I have also seen banks and other major companies use ML to tag and categorize customer questions with solutions. This allows the system to build an automatic knowledgebase over time that contains every question a customer has ever asked, with the correct solution.[4] This is extremely useful and can then be connected to a chatbot or used by a human to help the customer.

It's clear that although ML is a complex subject, it does have some very real and useful business applications. Cloud-based services are making it easier to experiment and deploy these solutions and I'm sure that it will feature as an important technology trend in the 2020s.

CHAPTER THIRTY EIGHT

HOW PREDICTIVE ANALYTICS AND OPTIMIZATION MODELS CAN HELP YOUR BUSINESS

APRIL 6, 2021

Predictive analytics has been around for decades, but as data storage has become cheaper and computers more powerful it is a strategy that can now be used by any company. In fact, I first remember being directly involved in this when I worked on a project to help an Indian credit card company back in 2006. They wanted to predict which customers would struggle to pay their bills. At the time it seemed like magic because the data analysts were so good at identifying which customers needed help.

Now it's easier, faster, and you don't need to be a mathematics graduate to explore the data and create 'what-if' scenarios.

In addition to my own credit card example, here are some scenarios where predictive analytics can play an important role:

1. **Fraud prevention:** pattern detection can highlight unusual interactions or transactions by your customers. We have all been called by our bank warning about a suspicious spending pattern–this is how they create those warnings.

2. **Optimize marketing:** predict who your best customers will be and focus more attention on them or determine where cross-sell opportunities might exist with existing customers. Using data to sniff out new opportunities.

3. **Improve Operations:** airlines and hotels predict when they will be quiet and automatically offer reduced prices for those rooms or flights–and conversely increase the price when popular. A predictive analytics engine will create the insight that allows this automated pricing to take place.

4. **Risk reduction:** credit scoring is a great example. By connecting together as much financial information about a potential customer as possible, such as income, bills, debts, and other liabilities, it is possible to estimate if you can extend credit to this customer.

One example that has become very popular in recent years is very similar to my experience in India and is focused on subscription companies. Subscriptions are no longer just for magazines–people are paying a monthly fee for their TV streaming service, mobile phone service, and Internet at home. It's now a very common business model to charge customers a monthly fee to access a service.

These companies can use predictive analytics to identify which customers are about to cancel their subscription. This can be based on behavioral insights–

exploring how customers used the service just before they previously left and matching this experience against present customers. This is why you might be thinking about leaving your mobile phone provider and then they contact you offering a special price if you lock yourself to their service for the next year.

Optimization models work in a similar way, often in parallel with predictive analytics, but they are really a mathematical model of your business, or a specific process. You can define input and outputs and can then experiment with scenarios that modify how the business operates. Rather than just predicting change, it allows for experimentation and then will create a prediction of the outcome of this change to the process.

Both these tools are extremely powerful and work across almost all businesses. Every company leader would like to be able to predict what their customers will do next. With these analytical tools you can almost get there.

CHAPTER THIRTY NINE

PREDICTIVE ANALYTICS

APRIL 13, 2021

Artificial intelligence (AI) and predictive analytics are becoming more important for more businesses today, but if you are not familiar with the mathematical models how do you understand the opportunities? What we are really exploring is the power to predict what your customers will do in the future, based on their previous behavior and other variables.

That sounds simple, but what are some real-world examples of how this can work?

Think about a bank with millions of credit card customers. The collections function at the bank is responsible for chasing customers who don't pay their bills. There will be a significant investment in this process, in addition to the problem of not actually receiving the cash on time. What if you could use predictive analytics to look at customer behavior and predict which customers are going to have a problem paying on time this month?

If you can step in and offer help to the customer before they default then it's likely that you can not only ensure that the payment will happen, but you have also dramatically improved the customer experience–that customer will feel far more loyal to a bank that helps them out.

There is a similar effect on subscription businesses too. This is when the customer is paying a fee every month to access a service. Maybe it's a magazine or Netflix, or their mobile phone contract. There will often be certain behaviors displayed by customers that are about to leave their subscription. Perhaps their movie watching dramatically declines as they start using a rival service or their phone use ceases when they were previously a regular user.

In this case there is the opportunity for a company to step in and offer a deal or package that will convince the customer to stay, even though the predictive analytics has identified that this customer is highly likely to stop using the service. If Netflix calls and says 'Would you commit to another year with us if we give you a 20% discount?' many customers are likely to respond to the offer.

We are seeing AI deployed in many other areas[1], such as intelligent automation and chatbots, and many of these solutions do work well, but there have been some disastrous implementations which makes many executives wary.[2]

I would step back and separate out the intelligence needed for predictive analytics from the more general AI used in direct customer interactions. You can use analytics to develop and train your internal team by using the system to identify weakness and areas that need improvement.[3] Not so you can exert more control, but so you can support the team and help them to improve faster.

Every company would love to predict what their customers will do next. Predictive analytics can give you the partial ability to do this. Customers will sometimes take random actions, but in most cases you can apply their previous behavior to an algorithm that also factors in environmental variables–the weather today, the traffic, special events taking place.

Retailers can form a much more supportive relationship with customers by knowing what they need and when. It can even create proactive opportunities where brands can suggest ideas to their customers. How many more cold beers could a retailer sell if they reach out to fans of beer automatically based on their previous spending patterns and the knowledge that a major football match will take place in the next few days? Predicting demand can create opportunities.

I believe that all companies across all industries will be using these tools to get closer to their customers. Brands that are not exploring the data they have will look extremely old-fashioned and will eventually fail. Who could now imagine what is special about a discount if it applies to every customer?

CHAPTER FORTY

SALESFORCE WILL LEAD CRM INNOVATION IN THE 2020S

APRIL 21, 2021

I remember studying Customer Relationship Management (CRM) at university. Back then the idea of CRM was really in its infancy and during the 1990s companies such as SAP, Siebel, and Oracle dominated the market.

As I started working within IT and becoming more senior in the companies I worked for, I noticed that CRM was always evangelized by those who stood to earn from the implementations, but the users rarely enjoyed using it. In fact, many of the users I met thought that it offered them no value at all and was a drain on their time.

This was when software would be individually installed on each PC so it often meant that each user needed another PC and that was another headache for the IT support team to manage. Often these systems gathered dust as the users built their own CRM inside Microsoft Excel.

Companies were spending a lot of money on CRM licenses that were not used and yet they also had to spend more supporting the systems. It was a mess.

It really took the launch of Salesforce in 1999 to change this. The founder, Marc Benioff, supported a cloud model from the start. He called it software-as-a-service and SaaS become a recognized delivery model for software. He was probably the first to start talking about a platform-as-a-service. Benioff pioneered the idea that users could pay for software as they use it, rather than needing to buy licenses up front.

From the early days, what was different about Salesforce was that you didn't need a lot of local infrastructure to run it—everything could just be managed remotely—and it was designed to actually be useful.

Spin forward to today and companies like Siebel are no longer around, bought by Oracle 15 years ago.[1] All the CRM majors now operate using cloud-based platforms demonstrating that Salesforce was right all those years ago. Salesforce is now the global CRM giant with revenues exceeding that of SAP, Oracle, and Microsoft's CRM platform all together.[2]

Now Salesforce not only leads the market in terms of revenue, but their reputation for innovation and great solutions exceeds the competition. In the past year, they have designed the Salesforce Sustainability Cloud, which allows companies to monitor their energy use and greenhouse gas emissions in real-time—essential for companies that are striving hard to improve their Environmental, Social, and Governance (ESG) measures.[3]

Salesforce is also leading the market in embracing flexible working options for their employees. They have worked with smaller cities[4] that are trying to attract new residents and have announced that the 9-5 shift in the office is dead.[5] From now on, the post-pandemic Salesforce does not insist on employees visiting their San Francisco office from Monday to Friday, they are judged by what they deliver, not by how much time they spend in the office.

All modern CRM systems help users to get leads, close deals, improve their productivity, and make better decisions, but Salesforce is constantly pushing the boundaries of innovation and redefining what it means to supply platforms to other companies. With such a strong product and market dominance it would require a very niche type of business to choose an alternative.

CHAPTER FORTY ONE

EVERYTHING-AS-A-SERVICE–HOW THE CLOUD IS DEFINING A NEW NORMAL

APRIL 27, 2021

The IT industry is growing fast, driven by an explosion in spending on post-pandemic digital transformation projects. Research from ISG indicates that global spending on IT and Business Process Outsourcing (BPO) in the first quarter of 2021 has grown by 11% since last year–$17bn of spending globally in a quarter.[1]

Where this gets really interesting is the numbers focused on cloud-based services. Of that entire $17bn, $10bn of it was spent in the cloud, reflecting a 15% year-on-year increase. The first quarter of 2020 was not really affected by the Covid-19 pandemic because most European and American lockdowns did not start until the middle of March, so these growth numbers really reflect a pre-pandemic state. With so much "new normal" investment now going into technology it is likely that growth will accelerate this year.

The advisory company McKinsey published a major report suggesting that recovery from the pandemic will be digital.[2] McKinsey suggests that IT spending is moving away from five-year-plans and traditional investment in infrastructure and into the cloud. Modern organizations need agility and this is exactly what the cloud can offer.

Many executives have been wary of buying cloud-based services. They wanted systems in-house so they can exert more control and have less data out there in the Internet. Now it seems that the opposite is true. Companies that cannot change quickly are now the ones that look risky. Buying services from the cloud, as and when your company needs them, allows you to pivot and reinvent how your company works with no infrastructure spending required.

Resilience is one of the key themes of the post-pandemic business environment. Organizations need to be able to change quickly–who could have imagined the challenges of 2020 as we were celebrating the end of 2019? The companies with rigid infrastructure plans may no longer even exist.

But how do you catch up? If you have spent years being wary of cloud-based services then how can you suddenly embrace it and what are the practical steps you need to take now?

First, it's likely that the pandemic has changed everything for your business so accept this. Accept that agility can be achieved with security–you don't need to trade one feature against the other. It's just that your security needs to be planned and managed differently to that old system.

Second, doing nothing is not an option. You cannot take your business into a digital future with the tired infrastructure that used to work well enough before the pandemic. Even if it looks like things are returning to normal, planning for the ability to manage events like this must be integrated into every aspect of your business processes. Creating the flexibility to change quickly is now essential.

I'd recommend finding a partner to help. Yes, you could just call up Azure or AWS and get a contract ready without hiring consultants, but there are many different clouds, some can remain private rather than public, and there are dozens of different cloud management systems–it's a whole new world and your existing internal skills may not be adequate to choose wisely.

Find an expert you trust and ask three questions:

1. **What is the opportunity?** Remove all the IT jargon and explain what my company can gain by adopting a cloud-based approach to infrastructure and services?

2. **What does it cost?** What are the various options for management systems and using a public or private cloud service? Are there different levels of service that would all work?

3. **Will you vanish after the implementation is complete?** Microsoft generally update their Azure system several times a day. You ideally want a partner that can stick around and offer advice on what's coming soon, which new features might help the business, how to improve security?

Most cloud services are pay as you go–you don't need to invest millions upfront in huge capital costs. This means that you can experiment more, you can try new ideas and services. Mistakes will be small. You can try a new service and cancel it if it doesn't work out.

You have an opportunity to build a new organization that is far more agile and more innovative. Why not seize it now?

CHAPTER FORTY TWO

ROBOTIC PROCESS AUTOMATION– HOW TO GET STARTED?

MAY 25, 2021

Forrester Research recently published their latest Wave analysis on Robotic Process Automation (RPA).[1] The research measures the strategy of each RPA supplier–marking each as weaker or stronger– then compares this to the actual present-day offering. So there is no judgement based on hype or what might be coming in the future.

The good news is that none of the major suppliers have a weak strategy and weak offering–all the companies are offering an attractive service. However, even the Forrester summary lists fourteen different suppliers and half a dozen of them are categorized as leaders–how do you get started with so many options?

First, you need to find some advice from someone that has already delivered RPA projects, so they can brief you on what is possible and which of the suppliers might be best for your specific problem. This is where a company like IBA has a great advantage because they have delivered hundreds of RPA solutions using all the leading software–so this is a great way to start.

Many executives start by directly approaching the leading RPA software companies, describing their problem, and seeing if the supplier can quickly come up with a pilot project that demonstrates their approach to building a solution.

The advantage is that this approach is free, but the big disadvantage is that once the pilot has been built then you will be locked into the solution and software offered by this company alone–it is unlikely that you can encourage several software companies to all build pilots. They will invest the time and effort in building an initial solution only if there is a strong chance that it will help them win the project.

For all these reasons I do believe that it makes sense to ask a trusted systems implementer for advice before you go to the software companies. If they have delivered many different systems then they will know the advantages and disadvantages of each system and how it might work for your solution.

A few more general points I would suggest are:

1. **Do your research:** do check what analysts like Forrester and HfS are saying about the RPA suppliers–the analysts have insight into how the market is developing.

2. **Use the trials:** you may be able to try out trial versions of various systems, just to get a feel for the strengths of each system.

3. **Experiment:** don't lock yourself entirely in with a single vendor right from the start. Try out some small projects with competing systems just to see what your team finds most useful.

4. **Workshop:** use workshops to really define what needs to be automated, what could be achieved, how long would it take? Create a plan that also has a benchmark–you know what will be improved and by how much.

RPA can appear to be a complex and expensive investment and it is easy to get locked in with a single supplier unless you take steps at the start of your journey to experiment and define how you want to use RPA. Do some research, think carefully about the type of solutions your business needs and then work with an experienced partner to select the best option. There are a lot of choices in the market right now, as the Forrester research shows, but sometimes you may need a niche player rather than the market leader. It's much easier to venture on this journey if you talk to someone that has already implemented RPA solutions in real companies.

CHAPTER FORTY THREE

RPA—SHOULD YOU ALLOW CITIZEN DEVELOPERS?

JUNE 17, 2021

I recently recorded a video discussion with the Robotic Process Automation (RPA) team[1] at IBA Group and the industry analyst Peter Ryan.[2] Our focus was RPA and how it can be applied to help companies reduce repetitive tasks.

One of the most interesting aspects of the discussion was the contrast between professional or citizen developers. I believe that many people exploring an RPA solution are doing so because they want to create a more agile process within their organization. This requires flexibility and the ability to change—therefore it makes sense for the team using the system to learn some basic coding and develop the ability to change and modify the automated processes.

However, as the IBA team noted, this also means that you can introduce errors. It's like earlier in my own career when I was coding. We had source code control systems, but they were extremely basic. It was fairly easy for one developer to make changes that impacted another member of the team.

This creates a dilemma. If you install an RPA system that can never be changed then there is no flexibility to modify the system, but if you allow the users to make changes then there is a risk that errors will be introduced. At the very least changes might be made and undocumented making it harder to support the system in future.

This is a similar problem to that faced by spreadsheet users. How many companies have a spreadsheet that holds everything together and only one person who understands the code? I've seen it many times in different organizations I have worked with. I once worked for an investment bank that reported their trading activity each day using an Excel sheet that only one person understood. When he was on vacation we just had to hope the sheet worked.

Clearly this is not acceptable and the IBA arguments about citizen developers are designed to avoid the same mistakes being repeated.

I believe that professionals are going to need some coding skills though. If it is possible to setup a mirrored system environment then there can be a test bed available for trials and experimentation. The production system is tested and locked, so it can't easily be changed, but a matching test system can offer the end users the opportunity to try their coding skills.

This is a question of digital literacy. What is a normal level of digital literacy today? Nobody really questions the basics any longer. I can remember people adding skills such as Word and Excel on their CV. Now it's just accepted as normal that most people understand how to use basic business tools, email, and social media.

Will RPA be next? I suspect that this is likely. As companies across all industries find that individual employees can be far more productive if they use RPA to remove repetitive tasks it will become common for companies to specify during the hiring process that they give priority to people that already understand some basic coding and automation processing.

It means that lawyers, doctors, and accountants will all need some basic coding skills. Citizen developers will become an important way that companies can increase productivity, but as the IBA team warned, source code must be controlled. We can't stumble into a situation where processes can be changed by anyone at anytime.

CHAPTER FORTY FOUR

DIGITAL TRANSFORMATION IS NOW A NECESSARY (NOT JUST A DESIRABLE) STRATEGY

JULY 6, 2021

The Covid-19 pandemic has created a focus on digital transformation. One look at Google Trends easily demonstrates how this topic has grown in importance of the past year or so.[1] Some companies were forced to pivot quickly because of the pandemic— it prevented normal business activities and therefore immediate change was essential.

But many others are now exploring how to change and improve by accelerating all those plans and discussions around what might be nice "if we have the time." It's an exciting time because not only are so many companies exploring how technology can improve their business, but so many new technologies are emerging and being adopted by enterprises.

Regardless of industry, it will be difficult to ignore this wave of change. There will be many new market entrants in areas such as banking and finance because of how technology allows them to offer services via apps–rather than a traditional banking network with branches in every major town. Some industries will be entirely reshaped–look at how the auto industry is exploring the idea of a car as a service, rather than just focusing on selling more units.[2]

There are too many trends to effectively summarize where transformation will take place first, but I believe these five are critical and all executives need to be aware of how their business may be transformed by them:

- **Internet of Things (IoT):** sensors are everywhere now and offer the ability to improve how property or industrial plants are managed or the option to create digital twins, so maintenance costs can be reduced and resources targeted more accurately.
- **Cloud:** nobody buys software and installs a CD on their computer now. We all just pay for software as it is used, with services delivered online from the cloud. This concept is being applied across more and more services, but the 'as a service' concept is entirely driven by cloud computing.
- **Artificial Intelligence (AI):** this is transforming how brands interact with their customers. AI and Machine Learning are allowing companies to study their customer behavior in more detail, to spot trends and even predict future behavior.
- **Robotic Process Automation (RPA):** the use of robot agents to automate processes has matured in recent years and I believe this trend will continue to penetrate all industries,

leading to the point where RPA skills become common digital literacy—like knowing how to write an email today.

- **Resilience:** although not strictly one single subject this combines cloud systems, information security, and business processes to create a more flexible and resilient organization capable of continuing to operate even during challenging situations—such as a global pandemic.

As indicated by the final point, there may be a need to combine several different technical areas to create transformation. However the point is that this can no longer be avoided. Transformation is no longer a desirable future state. It is now essential for long-term survival. No company can afford to wait for the next pandemic to arrive without any plan for remote working and other resilience measures.

CHAPTER FORTY FIVE

WHY BLOCKCHAIN MAY BE AN OPPORTUNITY FOR YOUR BUSINESS

JULY 26, 2021

In 2010 the software developer Laszlo Hanyecz used ten thousand bitcoins to buy two pizzas.[1] It is widely considered to be the first actual transaction of goods or products where payment was in bitcoin. Many in the IT industry now celebrate May 22nd each year as the 'bitcoin pizza day.'

At the time, this quantity of bitcoin was worth about $41 (USD). When I checked the current value online in April 2021 those two pizzas would cost $541 million. Quite a difference—hopefully Laszlo held on to some bitcoin rather than buying more pizzas.

Bitcoin still hasn't really gone mainstream. It's more like gold—an asset that people invest in rather than use to make purchases. What is really interesting about bitcoin though is that it is the first example of a global currency that uses a blockchain to keep track of who owns what. But what is blockchain technology and why should business leaders be more aware of the opportunities it may offer to their company?

In 2016 Don and Alex Tapscott published their book Blockchain Revolution, that both explained and defined blockchain and the possibilities it offers.[2] In the book they said:

"The blockchain is an incorruptible digital ledger of economic transactions that can be programmed to record not just financial transactions but virtually everything of value."

So in short, blockchain is a ledger that cannot be adjusted. It always maintains a record of every change. Records cannot be edited or deleted, only new ones can be added. Clearly the application of blockchain to bitcoin was logical, because of the need to trace financial transactions, but the same concept could equally be applied to other business problems–such as the need for a logistics company to track millions of parcels globally.

To understand the principle of how it works, let's think about a typical step-by-step blockchain transaction:

1. A transaction is requested–perhaps a payment from one person to another.

2. The requested transaction is sent to a peer-to-peer (P2P) network of computers known as nodes. The nodes can all talk to each other and all are aware of all requests–every node will be updated.

3. The nodes validate the user status and the requested transaction is applied.

4. Once validated the transaction is added permanently to the blockchain in a way that can never be changed. Note that transactions can only ever be added to the chain–previous actions cannot be deleted.

5. The transaction is validated and completed.

As a distributed database of transactions, a blockchain is hard to beat. It is simple, very hard to corrupt or infiltrate, self-correcting, and transparent. Clearly in systems or processes where trust and transparency are important, blockchain works well. The problem is that most business leaders have only ever heard of bitcoin as a system designed using a blockchain—and as the pizza example shows, that feels a bit wild.

Other use cases are out there if you look.[3] The logistics company DHL has been building a system that tracks drugs from manufacturing to consumption—cutting costs and improving trust and security in the drug production process. DHL has been working with management consultants from Accenture to establish this blockchain-based track-and-trace serialization system in six global regions. The system is now populated with more than 7 billion unique pharmaceutical serial numbers, and is handling more than 1,500 transactions per second.

The World Wildlife Fund has been exploring how to use blockchain to ensure that the seafood served in shops and restaurants really comes from where the vendor claims. This is because consumers are increasingly calling for fully-traceable seafood that does not come from illegal fisheries or those that engage in human rights abuses—especially in the case of fish such as tuna. Both wholesale and retail seafood buyers have been asking for improvements in transparency and traceability to reduce the risk of their brands being associated with illegal activities. The blockchain system can provide supply chain transparency and therefore the traceability that retailers and consumers want.

Additionally, food producers and retailers including Dole, Nestlé and Walmart have been using blockchain to track food production from the farm to the fork. The

United Nations has been exploring blockchain solutions to the problems of child trafficking and jewelers are using blockchain to ensure that the diamonds used in their jewelry is conflict-free.

Blockchain is moving away from the volatile reputation of bitcoin. With trusted organizations, such as the UN and WWF, rolling out major blockchain-supported initiatives and global logistics carriers finding value in the concept, it's time for more companies to explore how blockchain might work for them.

CHAPTER FORTY SIX

GARTNER SUGGESTS THE INTERNET OF BEHAVIORS WILL TRANSFORM IOT IN 2021

AUGUST 3, 2021

The industry analyst Gartner recently published their guide to the top strategic technology trends we need to be aware of in 2021.[1] One key trend I noticed when reading the document was how they believe that the world we presently talk of as the Internet of Things (IoT) is evolving into the Internet of Behaviors (IoB).

I'm not sure if the Gartner name will catch on as it has taken many years for the industry to even accept and understand IoT, but it's interesting to observe how they believe the IoT will develop to capture the digital dust everyone now leaves.

I think that perhaps 'digital breadcrumbs' is an even better description because it is this trail that advertisers are constantly following now. Gartner suggests that: "[this] information can be used by public or private entities to influence behavior. The data can come from a range of sources, from commercial customer data to social media to facial recognition, and as more and more data becomes available, the IoB will capture increasing amounts of information."

Gartner is really describing a world where almost all our actions are measured by sensors and recorded—for private or public use. I know that I am often surprised by how much data my iPhone captures without me even asking for it. I can see how far I walked, how many floors I climbed, how many steps I took and an exact map of where I have been—and that's all captured by default without me needing to setup any specific monitoring apps.

Insurance companies today are often asking drivers if they can monitor car use in real-time. The advantage for the driver is that the insurance can be priced more competitively if the driver can prove that they drive carefully and rarely drive at night. This ability to price risk more accurately also works better for the insurer. However, if the insurance company is cross-checking driver location against known locations of crimes in partnership with the local police then is that an invasion of personal data or a useful civic duty?

I recently wrote another article for IBA about the development of digital twins into healthcare—I think that this is going to be a dramatic move forward in how sensors inside the IoT are used, but the question of privacy remains.[2]

For example, if I know I have a heart problem and my cardiologist creates a model of my heart so he or she can compare feedback from my real heart with the digital twin in real time then this has tremendous potential for my health. My doctor should be able to use the model to predict any problem before it happens, but does a private company or government now have access to a real-time model of my heart?

To my mind, what Gartner is describing as an evolution from IoT to IoB is really this transition from being aware of what we are sensing and collecting and then moving into an environment where everything is monitored by default. Our health, our finances, our travel . . . every interaction. Everything.

As the insurance example indicates, there can be serious consumer benefits, but strong oversight is required for the public to trust these systems and all governments should stay well away from citizen data—but I doubt that is going to happen. Unless people are aware of what is about to happen.

CHAPTER FORTY SEVEN

CAN DIGITAL TWINS LEAD TO A DRAMATIC IMPROVEMENT IN HEALTHCARE?

AUGUST 10, 2021

'␣ve written in the past about Digital Twins on the blog, but interest in this area is soaring at present. Typically the solutions have been industrial–engine manufacturers using sensors to monitor engine performance or building plant managers overseeing intelligent buildings by using a twin. However, it is becoming increasingly common to see medical solutions exploring how digital twins can improve monitoring and solutions.

A recent edition of Venture Beat focused on this subject. They found dozens of individual examples where healthcare could be improved through the use of digital twins.[1]

I have been talking about remote health monitoring for a long time, in particular since Google acquired Fitbit. The opportunities for healthcare providers to start offering proactive medicine that monitors and helps patients, rather than waiting for a health problem to develop is really exciting.

But how are digital twins specifically influencing healthcare? Here are some of the most exciting examples featured in the Venture Beat focus:

- **Heart twins:** patients with heart problems that have a monitor or pacemaker fitted can transmit data back to a system that has already captured a digital version of their heart. This allows cardiologists to closely monitor any change in heart performance and any deterioration can be easily detected.
- **Symptom tracking:** Babylon Health has created a symptom tracker that can create a default twin that is then compared in real-time to data from a Fitbit or Apple Watch. It works with data such as health histories, a mood tracker, symptom tracker, and automatic capture from fitness devices. The digital twin can provide basic front-line information or help guide priorities and interactions with doctors to address more severe or persistent conditions.
- **Hospital twins:** Siemens has been exploring how to model and improve entire hospital departments. They are using workflow analysis, system redesign, and process improvement methodologies–for example to reduce the time required to treat stroke patients
- **Customer Service:** the TigerGraph database system tracks data from over 200 sources to create a complete health history of a patient when they contact their insurance company. This model helps the insurance company to

offer the best possible advice and makes service faster and more accurate.

- **Device twins:** hospitals are filled with complex equipment and Philips makes a large amount of the imaging devices we see in modern hospitals. They have started using digital twins of all their major hospital-based systems so they can improve maintenance and increase system availability.

These are just a few examples. The concept of digital twins is simple to understand, but as is becoming clear from all these healthcare examples, the opportunity to apply these ideas is now moving far beyond the classic engineering case studies.

Proactive healthcare is still in its infancy. Millions of consumers are now using complex sensors, such as the Fitbit and Apple Watch, but industries such as health insurance are only just beginning to see that investment in proactive monitoring can reduce their costs in the long term by improving health outcomes. The use of digital twins in healthcare is exciting, but will it eventually result in complete digital copies of our entire body? You might be getting a warning from your digital twin every time you drink a beer in future!

CHAPTER FORTY EIGHT

RPA: THE NEXT CHAPTER IN THE AUTOMATION STORY

AUGUST 18, 2021

recently participated in a really interesting discussion[1] on Robotic Process Automation (RPA) with the industry analyst Peter Ryan[2] and two of the team from IBA Group. Dimitri Denissiouk, is the Managing Director at IBA South Africa and Sergey Zlobich, is a Project Manager at IBA Group in Minsk.

I recently wrote about one part of the discussion–on citizen developers–you can read that article here.[3] I wrote that before the video was edited and published so I wanted to contribute another blog now that comments on the broader discussion.

It's worth saying right from the start that this was a very practical discussion. There are many webinars and debates that explore the theories around RPA and automation more generally, but this one dives straight into the pros and cons of working with RPA.

Dimitri sets the tone in his comments on the benefits of RPA. He said: "There are even less obvious benefits that RPA can bring, for instance reducing the risk because otherwise you would need to integrate two business applications and this is the risk of an impact on the existing environment. RPA projects are generally low risk and non-invasive. They don't disturb existing systems. Another non-obvious benefit is minimizing the exposure to sensitive data because now the robot works with the documents that may contain some private or sensitive data instead of humans so there is less risk of exposure to this data."

I liked this approach. Instead of just focusing on the obvious benefits, Dmitri really explored the question in more detail.

Sergey emphasized the non-invasive nature of RPA when he said: "I would like to add that we all think of RPA of as a tool to improve some existing business processes and make them better, smoother, but actually the technology also allows to introduce a brand new customer experience. It is faster than usual human processing. With a usual business process, it would be submitting requests and then after some time coming with a response that could be implemented the same time. I mean with a short waiting time, which is measured in seconds instead of hours, so that is also a great benefit that technology can provide."

The citizen developer debate was covered in my earlier blog, but Sergey continued the theme when talking about the need to create an RPA center of excellence inside the business. He said: "Let's make it short. When we are talking about a Center of Excellence, we should not think about a fixed structure. It's an evolution. And in the very beginning of that evolution, it is very reasonable to involve some external vendors who will bring their expertise to help set it up fast and to a minimal required level. But then, ideally, I think that each organization should try to make it in-house. I like the idea of a hybrid center of excellence. When you have some people in the center of excellence in-house and some are offshore developers, that should work and that is perfectly fine."

As we summed up the potential future for RPA, Peter made some interesting points. He said: "There's going to be a lot more development in in terms of that unattended element and the ability to learn from what previous tasks have been. Equally, I think that automation is going to be a lot more straightforward, not just for the individuals that implement the solutions for a client, but also for those who manage them. I think they're going to be a lot more intuitive, a lot more user friendly to the point where somebody who perhaps doesn't have a great development or technology background will be in a position to administer them."

That sounds like an exciting future. RPA that anyone can use. For now though, it's probably best to keep calling the experts and all my fellow panelists on this discussion really contributed some great ideas—check out the link below.

CHAPTER FORTY NINE

FINDING A PARTNER WITH GENUINE RPA EXPERIENCE–NOT JUST HYPE

AUGUST 25, 2021

I hosted an interesting discussion on my CX Files podcast recently.[1] It featured Alex Mead, a customer service director based in Bahrain. Alex has often mentioned on LinkedIn that he doesn't believe that any of the customer experience (CX) experts named on all the various 'top 50' lists actually know much about CX.

When I talked to Alex it became clear that he does have a valid point, but there are many types of expert. There are analysts, advisers, trainers, coaches, and people on both the buy side and sell side of the industry. I think that everyone in all these different areas has different expertise that they can bring to the table. The point is really that an 'expert' should only focus on the areas where they have genuine expertise and experience–not start handing out certification and courses.

I was thinking about this recently when I recorded a discussion about Robotic Process Automation (RPA) with the team at IBA Group. You can watch the discussion here on YouTube and I think it was a useful contribution to the understanding of RPA.[2]

RPA is one of those tech subjects that has been hyped for years. If you look at Google searches for information on RPA over the past 5 years, then you can see that interest has tripled during that time.[3]

It took until 2019 for business journals like Forbes to finally start declaring that RPA has moved from being mostly hype to now being an important business tool.[4] But there is still a lot of confusion around—that's partly because there are so many competing vendors, but also many of those promises about automation were inflated.

What I find interesting is that many IT managers exploring RPA do some basic research then call up a vendor directly and ask if they can manage a pilot—just to prove what is possible. This is a classic approach to testing out a new technology because it's low cost and risk-free, but it does lock you into a single vendor.

If that pilot works then that RPA vendor will get the business. But during the process of running that initial pilot the IT manager might find that another vendor looks more suitable—but they aren't in the room. It's a natural consequence of getting more familiar with the various vendors. They all have strengths and weaknesses.

It's not my job to directly promote IBA Group here on their blog—they have all their own information and marketing materials here anyway. However, the reason I connected the podcast on 'who is really an expert' to the RPA discussion on YouTube was because I was impressed with the underlying knowledge and experience of the IBA team.

They are not just producing flashy white papers or videos talking about the benefits of automation. In the discussion it was mentioned that they have implemented RPA systems for over 300 different companies and across several different vendors. So they know the strengths and weaknesses of the various RPA platforms and they have actually completed real implementations hundreds of times.

If I needed to explore RPA in 2021 and I didn't have much direct experience then I think I would rather get a team like this in to build a pilot and advise on the best platform, rather than randomly choosing a vendor just because they featured in a nice magazine article.

As my podcast suggested, sometimes it can be hard to work out who is a real expert and who is just great at marketing. In this case, the IBA team certainly rates highly on the ability to just get the job done.

CHAPTER FIFTY

A DATA REVOLUTION IS CHANGING HOW WE CAPTURE AND ANALYZE INFORMATION

SEPTEMBER 16 2021

One of the key changes in the way that most companies function today is their use of data. The Internet of Things (IoT) is allowing sensors to monitor supply chains and vast pools of customer behavior data can now be analyzed to spot trends or predict how they will behave in future.

But in the recent past, many systems have focused on the human, or manual, capture of information. A customer service agent might key in the name and address of a customer or the customer has to fill in several fields when checking their orders. Data has never been as important and yet if we are going to capture enough to make sense when analyzing it then we need a more industrial machine-focused approach.

Deloitte recently published research indicating that they believe there will be a transformation over the next 18-24 months in the way that companies capture and then manipulate data. Deloitte argues: "For their Machine Learning (ML) strategies to succeed, they [the companies] will need to fundamentally disrupt the data management value chain from end to end."[1]

Traditional databases have always focused on an array of records and fields, but this needs to be redefined if the data being captured can be used to help teach ML systems and subsequently be used by an Artificial Intelligence (AI) system.

Deloitte suggests three initial steps for executives thinking about how to improve their data capture and analysis:

1. **Capture and Store:** search all your legacy systems and databases for unstructured data that is not being analyzed at present and load it into a cloud-based database.

2. **Discover and Connect:** use cognitive data steward technology to create connections and highlight insights in the pool of data.

3. **Amplify ML Capabilities:** how can you use 5G and edge computing to decrease latency and increase the real-time capture of data across your entire system?

To my mind, this advice indicates that there is a dramatic change in the type of data being captured by modern companies. A database used to require strict formatting and rules about what could be captured—customer number, address, phone number etc. Now we are exploring the concept that anything and everything about how the customer behaves can be captured and analyzed—even down to how they browse on a website or how they physically move around inside a retail environment.

There are clearly some trends emerging:

- **Less clean data:** it will be more common to capture anything even if it doesn't fit inside a formatted database titled 'customer behavior.' This will be largely unstructured data that is captured automatically, rather than entered by a person.
- **More formats:** browsing data, images, video, sensor feedback, social media comments . . . data no longer needs to conform to a structured view and therefore it will come in many different formats and file types.
- **Real-time data:** as the Deloitte research indicated, the use of edge computing and 5G increases the ability to capture vast amounts of data in real-time. IoT sensors can use 5G to constantly send information, rather than waiting for the status of a sensor to be checked.

Cloud computing becomes essential in this environment. Not just to offer flexible storage, but also to ensure that a ML system is not inhibited by any local network issues or unreliability. It is certainly true that this reflects an enormous change in the way that data is gathered and analyzed—it's more automated and focused on real-time analysis, not just when a user sends a query to the database.

There is a revolution taking place in the capture, use, and analysis of data. It is being fueled by both the IoT and cloud and companies that don't review their data architecture now may well miss out if the Deloitte predictions on timelines are correct.

CHAPTER FIFTY ONE

PUBLIC CLOUD SERVICES SET TO ACCELERATE AS COMPANIES SEEK RESILIENCE

SEPTEMBER 27, 2021

Public cloud services are becoming such a go-to strategy for IT leaders that the industry analyst Garter estimates spending on these services will be close to half a trillion dollars in 2022 ($482bn).[1] The Covid-19 pandemic has accelerated a desire for companies to build resilience into their IT systems and a move to applications and data in public clouds has been the almost universal response.

But there are other trends helping the use of public cloud to accelerate. Garter identifies four specific trends in their own research. The four trends are: cloud ubiquity, regional cloud ecosystems, sustainability and carbon-intelligent cloud, and cloud infrastructure and platform service (CIPS) providers' automated programmable infrastructure. Let's consider each of these important trends in turn:

Cloud ubiquity

The cloud now underpins most innovation and resilience strategies. New systems and applications can be designed and tested without the need for upfront capital expenditure on architecture and data centers. The cloud in general has been proven to offer more flexibility, speed, resilience, and scalability than internal solutions—meaning that this is a solution that is better, but also more efficient and cost-sensitive.

Gartner forecasts end-user spending on public cloud services to reach $396 billion in 2021 and grow 21.7% to reach $482 billion in 2022. By 2026, Gartner predicts public cloud spending will exceed 45% of all enterprise IT spending, up from less than 17% in 2021. If almost half of all IT budget is focused on cloud services, that demonstrates how a cloud strategy is becoming ubiquitous.

Regional cloud ecosystems

Many regulated areas, such as public sector services or finance, are exploring how to avoid single-points of failure with their cloud provider and are therefore creating regional ecosystems. There are political and regulatory factors that are causing this, from differing data protection standards, even through to political protectionism.

Sustainability and carbon-intelligent cloud

Most executives now believe that climate change will have a future effect on their business. This is leading cloud providers to focus on how to offer carbon-neutral cloud services that can help companies achieve their ESG goals. This creates new challenges for infrastructure services, not least the energy use in cooling cloud data centers.

Automated programmable infrastructure

Machine Learning is increasingly being applied to the management of cloud services. This creates an environment where the cloud infrastructure is programmable and the management and operation can be more automated. This will change the routine administration of most cloud services.

Taken as a whole these four trends, and the financial investment figures detailed by Gartner, are extremely interesting and demonstrate that public cloud services have gone far beyond the tipping point where most executives start exploring their options.

The sheer ubiquity of cloud services in post-Covid highly resilient IT infrastructure cannot be ignored. Industries as diverse as customer service and e-commerce have all found that a public cloud offers dramatically more flexibility combined with resilience. Many cloud service providers have talked about the advantages of the cloud for several years now, but it has taken the Covid-19 pandemic for executives to really see that there is no alternative–any company that wants to build resilience in 2022 has to explore this option.

REFERENCES:

Chapter One
How Is Outsourcing Being Redefined For The Future?

1. www.itproportal.com/features/how-do-british-it-companies-use-outsourcing-to-europe-to-expand-their-skills-pool/

Chapter Two:
Why Won't Robots Replace Human Workers?

1. https://ibagroupit.com/
2. https://www.nytimes.com/2018/01/21/technology/inside-amazon-go-a-store-of-the-future.html
3. www.computerweekly.com/opinion/Robots-will-transform-not-replace-human-work
4. https://www.mckinsey.com/business-functions/digital-mckinsey/our-insights/where-machines-could-replace-humans-and-where-they-cant-yet

Chapter Three:
How The Robots In Your Home Are
Creating New Opportunities

1. https://www.mediapost.com/publications/article/302663/north-american-consumers-to-have-13-connected-devi.html

Chapter Four:
AI Is Bringing Brands And Consumers Closer Together

1. https://blog.adext.com/en/applications-of-artificial-intelligence

Chapter Five:
When Will Your HR Team Start Learning To Code?

1. https://www.forbes.com/sites/louisefron/2018/10/14/three-future-workplace-realities-you-must-be-prepared-for/#65d38047500e

Chapter Six:
How Tech Plays An Important Role
In Delivering Great CX

1. https://blog.ibagroupit.com/?p=2054
2. cxfiles.libsyn.com/andrei-lepeyev-iba-group
3. https://ibagroupit.com

Chapter Seven:
How Do You Understand What Customers Will Want
In The Future?

1. https://ibagroupit.com/en/newsroom/news/cxoutsourcers-04-04-19.html
2. https://www.slideshare.net/MarkHillary/profiling-the-consumer-of-the-future

Chapter Eight:
How Is Artificial Intelligence
Developing In The Enterprise?

1. https://www.forbes.com/sites/robertadams/ 2017/01/10/10-powerful-examples-of-artificial-intelligence-in-use-today/#2ab4eddc420d
2. https://j.mp/3kCMfli
3. https://www.vanityfair.com/news/2017/03/elon-musk-billion-dollar-crusade-to-stop-ai-space-x

Chapter Nine:
How Is RPA Innovation Taking Shape?

1. blog.ibagroupit.com/?p=2054
2. https://www.horsesforsources.com/RPA-BigThree_070318
3. https://bpmtips.com/rpa-tools-list-2018/
4. https://www.horsesforsources.com/ antworks_030619
5. https://www.ant.works/

Chapter Eleven:
How Do I Choose A Cloud Management Platform?

1. https://onapp.com/files/whitepapers/Neovise-Choosing-the-Right-Cloud-Platform.pdf

Chapter Twelve:
Everest Reports On A Complex And Competitive RPA

1. https://www.prweb.com/releases/everest_group_ issues_latest_assessment_of_rpa_technology_ vendors_as_market_becomes_increasingly_ complex_competitive/prweb16414734.htm

Chapter Thirteen:
What Are The Top Cloud Management Platforms?

1. https://blog.ibagroupit.com/?p=2191
2. https://www.itprotoday.com/performance-management/top-10-cloud-management-platforms-0
3. https://www.evaluatorgroup.com/

Chapter Fifteen:
A Renewed Focus On Cloud Security

1. https://www.geekwire.com/2019/amazon-capital-one-face-lawsuits-massive-hack-affects-106m-customers/
2. https://www.cio.com/article/3267571/it-governance-critical-as-cloud-adoption-soars-to-96-percent-in-2018.html
3. https://www.theglobeandmail.com/business/commentary/article-the-capital-one-breach-proved-we-must-rethink-cloud-security/

Chapter Sixteen:
Emerging Competition in European IT Outsourcing

1. https://emerging-europe.com

Chapter Seventeen:
The Soft Skills You Need To Work in DevOps

1. https://blog.ibagroupit.com/2019/09/why-should-i-be-thinking-about-devops/
2. https://techbeacon.com/devops/4-essential-soft-skills-every-devops-team-needs

Chapter Eighteen:
Cloud Spending

1. https://blog.ibagroupit.com/2019/09/a-renewed-focus-on-cloud-security/
2. https://en.wikipedia.org/wiki/General_Data_Protection_Regulation
3. https://blog.ibagroupit.com/2019/08/what-are-the-top-cloud-management-platforms/

Chapter Nineteen:
Can RPA Break Free of The Hype Cycle?

1. https://www.ibtimes.com/uipath-layoffs-400-lose-jobs-despite-startup-hitting-7-billion-valuation-2852663
2. https://venturebeat.com/2019/10/25/ai-weekly-uipath-wants-you-to-know-its-job-cuts-are-strategic-despite-the-optics/
3. https://www.information-age.com/uipath-fires-hundreds-employees-rpa-market-crisis-123485825/#
4. cxfiles.libsyn.com/sarah-burnett-everest-group-peak-matrix-rpa-research
5. https://blog.ibagroupit.com/2018/12/rpa-has-truly-arrived/

Chapter Twenty:
Where Will Cloud Computing Go In 2020?

1. https://www.techrepublic.com/article/forrester-the-5-ways-cloud-computing-will-change-in-2020/

Chapter Twenty One:
Can Microsoft Take The Lead in RPA?

1. https://www.horsesforsources.com/RPA-forecast-2016-2022_120118
2. https://reports.valuates.com/market-reports/QYRE-Othe-1M188/global-robotic-process-automation-market-2025
3. https://venturebeat.com/2019/11/08/microsoft-has-entered-the-rpa-market-what-does-that-mean/
4. cxfiles.libsyn.com/sarah-burnett-everest-group-peak-matrix-rpa-research

Chapter Twenty Two:
Digital Twins Are More Than Just 3D Models

1. https://www.spar3d.com/news/education-events/conferences/putting-digital-twins-to-work-means-going-beyond-visualization/
2. https://geobuiz.com/summit-2020/
3. https://en.wikipedia.org/wiki/Digital_twin
4. https://sloanreview.mit.edu/article/how-digital-twins-are-reinventing-innovation/
5. https://trends.google.com/trends/explore?date=today 5-y&q=digital twin

Chapter Twenty Three:
Becoming Strategic With RPA: How Managers Are Missing The Value Argument

1. https://www.intelligentsourcing.net/strategic-steering-of-automation-a-total-value-of-ownership-framework/

Chapter Twenty Four:
IoT Use Will Triple By 2022–What's Changing?

1. https://www.mckinsey.com/industries/private-equity-and-principal-investors/our-insights/growing-opportunities-in-the-internet-of-things
2. https://www.engadget.com/amazons-blink-mini-camera-announcement-183048551.html
3. https://shopus.furbo.com/

Chapter Twenty Five:
IDC Suggests A Focus On Big Data And AI

1. https://www.alibabacloud.com/solutions/intelligence-brain
2. https://pt.wikipedia.org/wiki/Turbi

Chapter Twenty Six:
Why Is There Is A Global Boom For Mainframes And COBOL?

1. https://techcrunch.com/2019/09/12/the-mainframe-business-is-alive-and-well-as-ibm-announces-new-z15/
2. https://home.treasury.gov/policy-issues/cares
3. https://en.wikipedia.org/wiki/Prime_Computer
4. https://en.wikipedia.org/wiki/Cambridge_Z88
5. https://en.wikipedia.org/wiki/Apollo_11
6. https://en.wikipedia.org/wiki/COBOL
7. https://www.bloomberg.com/news/articles/2020-04-13/an-ancient-computer-language-is-slowing-america-s-giant-stimulus
8. https://en.wikipedia.org/wiki/DevOps

Chapter Twenty Seven:
DevOps Has Redefined How To Manage Mainframe Systems

1. https://www.linkedin.com/in/markhillary/
2. https://en.wikipedia.org/wiki/
   Siemens_Nixdorf_Informationssysteme
3. https://www.google.com/search?q=epos&rlz=
   1C5CHFA_enBR881BR881&sxsrf=ALeKk01XUG
   m9sLQIV5i_
   BlxO0iYdtsOFbA:1592399482947&source=lnms&tbm
   =isch&sa=X&ved=2ahUKEwjP0pWs9ojqAhVbH7kG
   HWcOB7MQ_AUoAXoECBEQAw&biw=1283&bih=669
4. https://en.wikipedia.org/wiki/DevOps
5. https://en.wikipedia.org/wiki/
   Agile_software_development
6. https://en.wikipedia.org/wiki/Waterfall_model
7. https://j.mp/3m7JNsL
8. https://www.linkedin.com/in/
   yuliya-varonina-1b1233160/
9. https://en.wikipedia.org/wiki/Prime_Computer
10. https://www.planetmainframe.com/2020/04/
    mainframe-systems-help-to-keep-things-going-
    in-a-pandemic/
11. https://en.wikipedia.org/wiki/IBM_Z
12. https://www.vox.com/policy-and-politics/2020/5/13
    /21255894/unemployment-insurance-system-
    problems-florida-claims-pua-new-york
13. https://blog.syncsort.com/2020/01/mainframe/
    6-industries-with-mainframes/
14. https://j.mp/3m7JNsL

Chapter Twenty Eight:
Data Science Is The New Rock & Roll

1. https://en.wikipedia.org/wiki/Data_science
2. https://www.weforum.org/agenda/2019/04/how-much-data-is-generated-each-day-cf4bddf29f/
3. www.digitaljournal.com/pr/4581792
4. https://analyticsindiamag.com/why-a-career-in-data-science-should-be-your-prime-focus-in-2020/

Chapter Twenty Nine:
Modernizing The Mainframe: Open Source Trends

1. https://www.linkedin.com/in/markhillary/
2. https://www.linkedin.com/in/sergey-beganski-816581b0/
3. https://ibagroupit.com/
4. https://www.openmainframeproject.org/
5. https://www.linuxfoundation.org/
6. https://www.zowe.org/
7. https://www.koco.com/article/unemployment-agency-blames-incompatibility-of-new-old-technology-for-claims-delays/32843810#

Chapter Thirty:
Seek Quick Wins With High Impact If You Want Data Analytics To Succeed

1. https://hbr.org/
2. https://hbr.org/2020/03/whats-the-best-approach-to-data-analytics

Chapter Thirty One:
Modernising The Mainframe: Open Source Summit And Trends

1. https://linuxinsider.com/story/the-linux-foundations-first-ever-virtual-open-source-summit-86754.html
2. https://www.inxpo.com/
3. https://www.expresscomputer.in/open-source/google-launches-new-kind-of-open-source-organisation/60345/
4. https://www.forbes.com/sites/adrianbridgwater/2020/07/13/how-open-source-software-gets-bootstrapped/#6b4ad2c4bf52
5. https://www.openmainframeproject.org/press/2020/06/24/open-mainframe-project-announces-major-technical-milestone-with-zowes-long-term-support-release
6. https://www.zowe.org/
7. https://www.linkedin.com/in/sergey-beganski-816581b0/
8. https://ibagroupit.com/
9. https://j.mp/3oa5NWz

Chapter Thirty Two:
Gartner Strategic Predictions For 2021: Seismic Change Coming Soon

1. https://www.gartner.com/smarterwithgartner/gartner-top-10-strategic-predictions-for-2021-and-beyond/

Chapter Thirty Three:
Gartner Strategic Predictions For 2021: Digital Disruption Is The Message For 2021

1. https://www.gartner.com/smarterwithgartner/ gartner-top-10-strategic-predictions- for-2021-and-beyond/
2. https://www.gartner.com/smarterwithgartner/7- digital-disruptions-you-might-not- see-coming-in-the-next-5-years/
3. https://en.wikipedia.org/wiki/Moore's_law
4. https://j.mp/3ibynD7

Chapter Thirty Four:
Covid Gives A Dramatic Boost To Digital Twins

1. https://blog.ibagroupit.com/2019/06/digital- twins-will-aid-digital-transformation-in-2020/
2. https://www.computerweekly.com/ news/252457997/IT-professionals-are- getting-ready-for-the-onset-of-digital-twins
3. https://www.computerweekly.com/ news/252491333/Nearly-half-of- firms-to-increase-investments-in-IoT- despite-the-impact-of-Covid-19
4. https://www.computerweekly.com/ news/252457997/IT-professionals-are- getting-ready-for-the-onset-of-digital-twins

Chapter Thirty Five:
How The IoT Creates A Need For Digital Twins

1. https://en.wikipedia.org/wiki/Digital_twin
2. https://en.wikipedia.org/wiki/Internet_of_things

3. https://sloanreview.mit.edu/article/
   how-digital-twins-are-reinventing-innovation

Chapter Thirty Six:
What's The Immediate Future For Chatbots And Voice Recognition?

1. https://j.mp/39Mm77e
2. https://j.mp/3AQvHSD
3. https://j.mp/2WeZHse
4. https://j.mp/3ALQZ3X
5. https://www.ibm.com/cloud/learn/
   natural-language-processing
6. https://www.ibm.com/cloud/
   learn/speech-recognition

Chapter Thirty Seven:
How Can Companies Benefit From Machine Learning?

1. https://www.ibm.com/cloud/machine-learning
2. https://blogs.oracle.com/datascience/6-common-
   machine-learning-applications-for-business
3. https://freshdesk.com/customer-
   support/machine-learning-optimizing-
   customer-support-blog/
4. https://www.zendesk.com/blog/
   machine-learning-used-customer-service/

Chapter Thirty Nine:
Predictive Analytics

1. https://www.forbes.com/sites/
   forbestechcouncil/2021/03/04/how-cognitive-
   virtual-agents-can-revolutionize-the-customer-
   support-industry/?sh=64e952a38dd5

2. https://www.cio.com/article/3586802/5-famous-analytics-and-ai-disasters.html
3. https://www.chieflearningofficer.com/2021/03/19/black-mirror-or-better-the-role-of-ai-in-the-future-of-learning-and-development/

Chapter Forty:
Salesforce Will Lead CRM Innovation In The 2020s

1. https://en.wikipedia.org/wiki/Siebel_Systems
2. https://en.wikipedia.org/wiki/Customer_relationship_management#CRM_market
3. https://www.greenbiz.com/article/salesforce-accenture-and-tipping-point-carbon-accounting
4. https://www.bizjournals.com/sanfrancisco/news/2021/02/09/salesforce-adds-fuel-to-cities-pursuit-of-remote-w.html
5. https://www.theverge.com/2021/2/9/22275304/salesfore-remote-work-9-to-5-workday-is-dead-flex-coronavirus

Chapter Forty One:
Everything-As-A-Service–How The Cloud Is Defining A New Normal

1. https://www-computerweekly-com.cdn.ampproject.org/c/s/www.computerweekly.com/news/252499093/Global-demand-for-IT-and-business-services-highest-ever-for-first-quarter
2. https://www.mckinsey.com/~/media/McKinsey/Business Functions/McKinsey Digital/Our Insights/How six companies are using technology and data to transform themselves/The-next-normal-the-recovery-will-be-digital.pdf

Chapter Forty Two:
Robotic Process Automation–How To Get Started?

1. https://www.uipath.com/resources/automation-analyst-reports/forrester-wave-rpa

Chapter Forty Three:
RPA–Should You Allow Citizen Developers?

1. https://ibagroupit.com
2. ryanadvisory.com/

Chapter Forty Four:
Digital Transformation Is Now a Necessary (Not Just A Desirable) Strategy

1. https://trends.google.com/trends/explore?date=today 5-y&q=/m/0g5r88p
2. https://www.volvocars.com/us/care-by-volvo/

Chapter Forty Five:
Why Blockchain May Be An Opportunity For Your Business

1. https://en.bitcoin.it/wiki/Laszlo_Hanyecz
2. https://www.amazon.com/Blockchain-Revolution-Technology-Changing-Business/dp/1101980133
3. https://www.techrepublic.com/article/6-ways-companies-are-using-blockchain-to-drive-value-right-now/

Chapter Forty Six:
Gartner Suggests The Internet Of Behaviors Will Transform IoT In 2021

1. https://www.gartner.com/en/ information-technology/trends/ top-strategic-technology-trends-iot-gb-pd
2. https://blog.ibagroupit.com/

Chapter Forty Seven:
Can Digital Twins Lead To A Dramatic Improvement In Healthcare?

1. https://venturebeat.com/2021/07/04/21-ways- medical-digital-twins-will-transform-healthcare/

Chapter Forty Eight:
RPA: The Next Chapter In The Automation Story

1. https://j.mp/3m3GJOb
2. https://www.linkedin.com/in/ peter-ryan-montreal/
3. https://blog.ibagroupit.com/2021/06/ rpa-should-you-allow-citizen-developers/

Chapter Forty Nine:
Finding A Partner With Genuine RPA Experience- Not Just Hype

1. https://cxfiles.libsyn.com/alex-mead-who- decides-on-who-is-really-a-cx-guru
2. https://j.mp/3m3GJOb
3. https://trends.google.com/trends/ explore?date=today 5-y&q=RPA

4. https://www.forbes.com/sites/
   forbestechcouncil/2019/12/18/the-rpa-hype-
   cycle-is-over-heres-the-reality/?sh=30a59a2866f8

Chapter Fifty:
A Data Revolution Is Changing How We Capture And Analyze Information

1. https://www2.deloitte.com/us/en/
   insights/focus/tech-trends/2021/
   disrupting-ai-data-management.html

Chapter Fifty One: Public Cloud Services Set To Accelerate As Companies Seek Resilience

1. https://www.gartner.com/en/newsroom/press-
   releases/2021-08-02-gartner-says-four-trends-
   are-shaping-the-future-of-public-cloud

APPENDIX 1

RPA: The Next Chapter In The Automation Story
June 8, 2021

RPA: The Next Chapter In The Automation Story
Panel Discussion (introduced by Irina Kiptikova)

We are going to talk about a very exciting technology that is transforming businesses and even our lives, that is Robotic Process Automation or RPA.

The panelists are two analysts working in the customer experience field and two IBA experts.

Mark Hillary is a British technology writer and analyst, based in São Paulo, Brazil. Mark contributes to the global media focused on technology and has written several books on technology. Mark advises national governments on technology policies and has advised the United Nations on the use of technology for development.

Peter Ryan is one of the foremost experts in customer relationship management. Peter received numerous prestigious awards in the customer experience field and is included in each iteration of the Nearshore Americas Power 50 influencers listings. In cooperation with Knowledge Executive, a specialized research & media house working with C-Level executives, Peter conducts annual vendor surveys to identify Top Offshore Customer Experience Delivery Points. This year, South Africa was selected as a number one BPO destination.

Therefore, we are going to discuss RPA in South Africa as a part of the generic RPA topic and I invited Dimitri Denissiouk, Managing Director at IBA South Africa, to help us explore the topic.

Sergey Zlobich, a Project Manager at IBA Group, will share a technical perspective on RPA, based on his many-year experience in RPA projects.

Mark Hillary

"The development as we move forward will be in the area of AI and machine learning. Training a bot can actually be unattended, more intelligent systems able to learn from repeated processes."

Peter Ryan

"Automation is going to be a lot more straightforward, not just for the individuals that implement the solutions for a client, but also for those who manage them. I think they're going to be a lot more intuitive, a lot more user friendly."

Dimitri Denissiouk

"There will be more cognitive capabilities in RPA, so it will be able to automate not only simple workflow processes, but more complex business scenarios and it will manage unstructured data or natural language, or perhaps it will do some data mining and analysis, and maybe predictive analysis."

Sergey Zlobich

"Software will write its own code, write itself on its own. Employees will say 'hey, this is something that could be automated' and it is automated automatically."

What are the benefits of RPA?

Mark:

I think that we've known about automation systems for a long time. We've seen workflow automation, but what's really kind of changed with RPA is the ease of creating the automated workflows, so you know it's very much focused on using a graphical user interface to train the agent or the bot in what needs to be automated, so that's one of the big differences here that it's much more simple now and really the business benefit is around reducing repetition, reducing mundane workflows, where I'm often writing about the customer service, customer experience space.

We see contact center agents that are often using multiple systems and transferring customer information from one system to another and traditionally this has been quite a manual, mundane repetitive process. There's the potential for introducing errors, so you're not only automating tasks and making it faster and simpler, and easier, but you're also reducing the possibility of introducing errors as well. So there's multiple benefits.

Peter:

South Africa was selected as the most favored offshore location by enterprise customer experience buyers and I think there was a number of reasons. They've been very active and very aggressive in their promotion to the key demand markets, that is the United Kingdom, North America, Australia, and New Zealand. That's one reason. I think another reason is the fact that there is a very strong reputation for quality in South

Africa: quality labor force, the willingness of the agents to be problem solvers and to go the extra mile and certainly a great cultural and linguistic affinity with the consumers that they tend to support now in terms of your question around the benefits of RPA. I think that Mark laid it out very nicely. I would say that from my perspective what I've been observing the length of time I've been in the contact center and the customer experience space.

Automation has had a series of stops and starts when I first got into this game in 2003-2004. There was talk that automation was going to kill the call center, was going to get rid of all the agents and everything was going to be automated, but very quickly we saw that the technologies were being deployed too aggressively without being stress tested properly and it sort of went into hibernation.

It's had a rebirth of sorts over the past several years and I think with very good validation too the solutions are much more apropos, they're much more realistic. And I think that the key benefit we're seeing now is taking the mundaneness of an agent interaction at least in the initial stages out of a telephone call or a digital interaction, and what it's doing is helping the workflow move a lot more quickly and a lot more efficiently. So, by the time you get to an agent, if you need to get to an agent after going through the automated interface, there's a much better chance that your issue will be resolved in a more expeditious fashion from the standpoint of automation.

I think that there's been some great strides, especially with the implementation of artificial intelligence and drawing that into the ability for automation to be able to interact more seamlessly, but the development continues and I think that the benefits are going to be seen for some time, especially as the competition in terms of the developers that are bringing the new solutions to the forefront, improve their solutions, and make them even more customer ready.

Dimitri:

Mark and Peter already talked about some of the obvious benefits. There are even less obvious benefits that RPA can bring, for instance reducing the risk because otherwise you would need probably to integrate two business applications and this is the risk of an impact on the existing environment, while RPA projects are generally low risk and let me call them non-invasive. They don't disturb existing systems. Another non-obvious benefit is like minimizing exposure to sensitive data because now the robot works with the documents that may contain some private or sensitive data instead of humans so there is less risk of exposure to this data.

Sergey:

I would like to add that we all think of RPA of as a tool to improve some existing business processes and make them better, smoother, but actually the technology also allows to introduce a brand new customer experience. It is faster than usual human processing. With a usual business process, it would be submitting requests and then after some time coming with a response that could be implemented the same time. I mean with a short waiting time, which is measured in seconds instead of hours, so that is also a great benefit that technology can provide.

Some companies complain that RPA is costly. Let's talk about the Total Cost of Ownership in relation to RPA. How do we make it lower?

Peter:

I think that the discussion around RPA is one that has been lingering for a long time, but I would put it like this. When you find a good RPA system, one that works really well,

one that has been stress tested and proves water tight, it'll pay for itself very quickly in terms of being able to route customer interactions, in terms of being able to solve some interactions upfront and effectively, what that means is that you're reducing the need for the human element and what we know is and I'm sure Mark can back this up that roughly speaking, the human element in a contact center accounts for 70 to 75 percent of cost, depending on the location that you might be in now. When you factor the opportunity of taking the human element out of the contact center and being able to replace some of that with an RPA solution, that certainly might have an upfront capital cost, but will be significantly lower over the long term. I really believe that that's a very compelling economic argument for deploying the solution, but the key here is to make sure that it's going to be an efficient solution, one that's going to work well, one that will obviously need tweaking and updating, but one that you can count on to get the job done, that will be a very cost effective play over the long term.

Mark:

Yeah, I would just say that, and it probably goes to Sergey, that about half of the TCO is probably your development and deployment of the system itself. You know you have ongoing licensing and maintenance costs afterwards, but the biggest chunk is to create it in the first place. So, I guess, working with the company that is implementing the system for you, and helping you to find the best vendor, you know, this kind of investment upfront in finding a great partner. Well, like IBA Group, for example, but this really does impact massively on the total cost of an RPA project.

Sergey:

As Mark said, I am usually on another side. When we are talking about the total cost of ownership, and we are saying that it is high, we always compare it with economical and with the business benefits we get from RPA implementation. And if that cost is not less than the benefits, that means probably that the business processes, which were implemented and automated, are not picked correctly, maybe they are not optimized enough or good enough to be automated. My idea is that for good implementation you should not think about having the total cost of ownership lower, you should think about making business benefits minus total cost of ownership bigger, so always try to focus on that, not on just minimizing the total cost of ownership.

Dimitri:

I agree with what you already said. I can just add that the total cost of ownership consists of multiple elements or factors. It is license fees, development costs, center of excellence, operating costs including OCR (optical character recognition), and maintenance of the platform, and also I can add business process maintenance. So, if you are looking to reduce or make it lower, then you need to analyze each of those elements, each of those factors, and see what can be done there. It's a holistic approach. For instance, with license fees, you can compare what different vendors provide or even go for a platform with zero license fees or operating costs. Some OCR tools have a pay-per-use model, which means the more documents you scan or recognize, the more you pay, but there are also open source engines. So it's really like a holistic approach.

What would you say is best: citizen developers or professional developers in relation to RPA?

Mark:

I think, this really depends on the kind of policies you've got within your organization, how you control source code, for example. I do think that, in general, we are moving towards an environment where professionals outside of the IT industry will need some sort of basic understanding of tools, like how to code a basic automation system. So we can imagine a future world where lawyers, accountants, doctors can learn how to automate processes that they previously couldn't have. But clearly, you have the problem of source code control. I mean, if you have a big enterprise and you've rolled out a system and then everybody in the company can just tinker around and play with it, then clearly it can introduce problems. It's a question of balance, how you control the system that's being used.

Peter:

I really couldn't disagree with what Mark said. I think that it's great to have a robust team of people who have got their own ideas in terms of how development has to go forward.

That's how we've seen some of the best innovations in technology over the course of the past two or three decades, and some of the huge leaps forward that we've all experienced as business people and consumers. At the same time, I think Mark is bang on in the sense that, unless there is some overriding control, in regards to how a community of developers is going to tinker and tweak around the edges. That could introduce more problems, so certainly encouraging innovation, encouraging, trying new things is absolutely essential, but making sure that there is some level of coordination is going to also be imperative.

Dimitri:

I would personally go for the Pro Developer Approach because for Citizen Developers developing of bots or automating the processes is not the main task. His or her focus will be shifted to main duties. Pro Developer is my primary task. And, moreover, the Pro Developer has more experience, obviously, so, the bots created by the Pro Developer will be more reliable or easy to maintain and less error prone. So I would say for Pro Developer.

Sergey:

I'm a little bit an interested party here. So, I am on the developer side. I can see benefits for both approaches and, actually, the main benefit in the Citizen Developer approach is that it is very fast. So, if a business person does know the business problem and can do programming, then he can create his bot in several days, maybe even hours, if it is a simple bot, and you will never get that speed with separate developers. You will need to get solution, design, budget, and time allocation and that is slower. But to advocate professional developers: all that steps are still required because when you create a good solution design, you usually ask some questions which you may not think about previously, and the questions or answers to the questions, could change the automation dramatically. So, instead of doing something very fast, you do the right thing slower and I think the second is better.

How about Centers of Excellence? Are they really needed? And if yes, should they be in-house or external?

Mark:

I think that what we're talking about here is changing the culture of an organization. If you are the CFO and you can see the potential for the organization of automating many individual processes, then you need a way to demonstrate that across the entire enterprise. I think that you definitely need a center of excellence to demonstrate the value of RPA. Personally, I would think that it could work internally or externally, but if you're going to do it externally, then you need to have a – again, like I was saying about the implementation,– you need a partner that you can rely on, and, maybe, an independent partner, not a partner that is tied to one particular RPA vendor, for example. So, if you've got a great partner, then you could do this externally. Otherwise, you know, clearly it's a kind of an evangelism role within the organization to show people what's possible.

Peter:

I think that some of the best innovations we've seen have come out of centers of excellence. And one of the things that I'm encouraged at, especially as I visit my friends in the CX technology industry, is to see so often that they have set up their own centers of excellence. Their own laboratories, in which they go out, they hypothesize, they construct, they test, and if it works – great, if it doesn't–they start over. The reality is, if you can have centers that are going to spend their entire time and are dedicated to developing the best possible solutions, whether it's automation or otherwise, I don't see anything wrong with that. I definitely agree with Mark that you should not exclude the possibility of working with outside partners that are in a position to bring perhaps solutions that the contracting organization might not have thought of. They can bring these to the table using an external organization that certainly has a great deal of merit in regards to making sure that a client gets the best possible technology that they're looking for, that's going to help them innovate, that's going to help them position themselves more competitively. But the reality is: the only way the industry is going to move forward, in automation or any other aspect of a technical solution, is by developing that critical mass around thought leadership, trying new ideas, going out, making sure that these ideas are given as much scrutiny as possible, that they work. Take them out as aggressively as you can, implement them as aggressively as you can. If they don't figure out and don't work, then start afresh.

Dmitri:

I think it's like continuing discussion on a Pro-Developer and Citizen Developer. Regardless if we have business user or professional developers who create support to automate some business processes, the question is who will own this bot. I mean, who will document it and maintain because in the future, if a business application changes the screen, this bot will stop working. So someone need to fix it. I believe that bots should not be owned by individual business users or pro-developers, but sure, they should be owned by the organization itself. Therefore, the organization needs a unit, which will own those bots, will govern them, do all the maintenance, document them, and maybe it will have some guidelines and standards, like all the bots should follow all new developments. Therefore, this unit is definitely needed in organizations. About external or in-house: I think, there is a mixture. The organization can have a hybrid center of excellence. That means some of the employees are in-house and some are from a vendor or external partner. In South Africa, it's like a standard. So each organization should work out its own way. I know that one big telecommunication group of companies of South Africa and southern Africa. They have around 80 employees in-house in the center of excellence and around 20 are external. So, this is like 80 to 20 proportion. But again, this is not a rule and each organization should check what works best for it.

Sergey:

Let's make it short. When we are talking about a Center of Excellence, we should not think about a fixed structure. It's an evolution. And in the very beginning of that evolution, it is very reasonable to involve some external vendors who will bring their expertise to help set it up fast and to a minimal required level. But then, ideally, I think that each organization should try to make it in-house, have an in-house center of excellence. I like the idea of a hybrid center of excellence. When you have some people in the center of excellence in-house and some are offshore developers, that should work and that is perfectly fine. But to my understanding, somebody should always be in-house.

How is RPA going to develop?

Mark:

I think that we see a difference between attended and unattended RPA, and the complexity of something that's simple for a human like looking at a document and understanding the information there is actually quite a complex process. You need to digitize the document, you need to extract all the information, you need to validate whether it makes any sense, is it correct. I think that you know the development as we move forward will be in the area of AI and machine learning, and being able to do those kind of things that are simple for a human when you're attending the RPA session and training a bot, so that more of it can actually be unattended, more intelligent systems able to learn from repeated processes.

Peter:

Everything Mark said, I think is bang on. There's going to be a lot more development in in terms of that unattended element and the ability to learn from what previous tasks have been. Equally, I think that automation is going to be a lot more straightforward

not just for the individuals that implement the solutions for a client, but also for those who manage them. I think they're going to be a lot more intuitive, a lot more user friendly to the point where somebody who perhaps doesn't have a great development or technology background will be in a position to administer them. And I also think that we're going to see those smart solutions that Mark referred to become much more customer friendly and I think we're going to see that the basic automated solutions that are handling customer management queries right now become much more complex in terms of the type of interactions they're able to drive, which is going to benefit everybody.

Dmitri

I concur with Mark and Peter, and I think that there will be more cognitive capabilities in RPA, so it will be able to automate not only simple workflow processes, but more complex business scenarios and it will manage unstructured data as an input or natural language or perhaps it will do some data mining and analysis, and maybe predictive analysis. And I think that all the RPA platforms will have machine learning and AI capabilities.

Sergey

Almost everybody said about some cognitive capabilities and I agree that it would be definitely one of the points. I think that another point could be when software would write its own code, write itself on its own. Several vendors already come to market with a solution that monitors user actions. They see repetitive actions across multiple users and after that they provide information on these actions. Once you have that information, it is very easy to actually write a business process. So that can also be done automatically. Ideally, there would be a system, which is watching the employees saying 'hey this is something that could be automated' and it is automated automatically.

Follow these links to watch or read the coverage of this entire panel discussion:

Video:
http://j.mp/RPAIBAGROUP

Written transcript:
https://blog.ibagroupit.com/2021/06/
rpa-the-next-chapter-in-the-automation-story/

The Digital CEO:
A Dozen Years Of IT Insight

by

Mark Hillary
© Mark Hillary and IBA Group Books 2021
All Rights Reserved

Published by IBA Group Books
Prague, Czech Republic

www.ibagroupit.com
https://blog.ibagroupit.com/

Published by IBA Group Books
Prague, Czech Republic

www.ibagroupit.com
https://blog.ibagroupit.com/